The Architecture of the American Summer

The Flowering of the Shingle Style

The Architecture of the American Summer

The Flowering of the Shingle Style

Introduction by Vincent Scully

The Temple Hoyne Buell Center
for the Study of American Architecture
Columbia University, The City of New York

Documents of American Architecture Series

General Editor: Robert A. M. Stern

The Architecture of the American Summer: The Flowering of the Shingle Style, introduction by Vincent Scully, 1989.

Special thanks to the National Endowment for the Arts and the L.C. and Margaret Walker Foundation, whose generous grants helped make possible the publication of this inaugural book in the series "Documents of American Architecture."

First published in the United States of America in 1989 by
RIZZOLI INTERNATIONAL PUBLICATIONS, Inc.
597 Fifth Avenue, New York, NY 10017

Library of Congress Cataloging-in-Publication Data
Scully, Vincent Joseph, 1920–
    The architecture of the American summer.

    Bibliography: p.
    1. Architecture, Domestic—Shingle style—United
States.   2. Architecture, Modern—19th century—
United States.   3. Vernacular architecture—United
States.   I. Title.
NA7207.S375   1989   728'.0973   86-42763
ISBN 0-8478-0769-X
ISBN 0-8478-0782-7 (pbk.)

Designed by H Plus, Inc.
Set in type by Trufont Typographers
Printed and bound in the U.S.A.

Contents

Acknowledgements

The Buell Center would like to thank the Design Arts Program of the National Endowment of the Arts and the L.C. and Margaret Walker Foundation for their support of this project.

The efforts of many people have gone into the making of this volume. The Buell Center would like to thank the staff of the Avery Architecture and Fine Arts Library at Columbia University, especially Angela Giral, Herbert Mitchell, Janet Parks, and Lisa Rosenthal; Tony Wrenn at the American Institute of Architects Archives in Washington, D.C.; Jack Perry Brown and Mary Woolover at the Ryerson and Burnham Libraries at the Art Institute of Chicago; Mary Schmidt at the Marquand Library at Princeton University; Cammie Naylor at the New-York Historical Society; Mosette Broderick and the Estate of Henry-Russell Hitchcock; Richard Longstreth; and David Dashiell of Venturi, Rauch and Scott Brown, Inc., for their efforts in supplying the many images reproduced in this book.

Steven Bedford contributed valuable information on several occasions. Research assistance was provided by Karl Bahr-DeLeon, Richard Cohen, Christopher Jarrett, and Robert Norden. Elizabeth Gerstein, the Assistant Editor, was largely responsible for pulling all of the pieces together. Ann ffolliott acted as Managing Editor.

Robert A. M. Stern

Foreword

by Robert A.M. Stern

With the publication of *The Architecture of the American Summer: The Flowering of the Shingle Style,* the Buell Center is pleased to inaugurate a series of publications, "Documents in American Architecture," bringing to the public's attention important material in the field of American architecture, some of it unknown or underillustrated in the original studies. Annotated and interpreted by leading scholars in the field, the "Documents" series is intended to create a setting in which specialists can share their knowledge and ideas with colleagues and the public, filling a gap between the frequently spatially-confined essay format and the full-fledged monograph. The series will take two directions: 1) the publication of hitherto unpublished original material, usually drawings or photographs; and 2) the re-publication of secondary material that can be found only in rare or unusual publications, frequently unavailable except in specialized archival collections.

The Architecture of the American Summer: The Flowering of the Shingle Style is a pictorial history further illustrating and expanding Professor Scully's epoch-making *The Shingle Style* of 1955, with some two hundred drawings of buildings culled from the vast number reproduced in the architectural periodicals of the period. Professor Scully's study has proved of central importance in the development of American architecture during the past generation, and it is hoped that this publication, with many new illustrations and with Professor Scully's thoughts on the subject some thirty years later, will respond to this longstanding interest and provide more documentation for it.

Professor Scully confined his original study to the Eastern seaboard and to the early and climactic years of the style. Here the lens is widened to take in the country as a whole and the entire range of the style in time. It also deals with various building types other than houses. While the Shingle Style found its principal expression in the design of single family houses, its freedom and flexibility lent itself to the design of other kinds of buildings, as well. Open plans and picturesque compositions were well suited to the hotels and country clubs typical of the new leisure. In addition, such diverse types as railroad stations and churches found appropriate form in the Shingle Style. Thus, new communities of buildings began to extend the architectural traditions of an earlier urbanism rather than proposing the stylistic diversity and compositional individualism so characteristic of mid-nineteenth century city development. The new Shingle Style towns and districts were village-like in scale and character and were typically resort communities physically and stylistically appended to Colonial settlements, as in Newport, Rhode Island, and East Hampton, Long Island, New York.

By the end of the nineteenth century, the flexibility and picturesque quality of the Shingle Style had become the representative expression of the ideal of a leisurely family life on the land. As this compilation demonstrates, it was adopted even by the normally high style academic aestheticist John Russell Pope. And, as Scully long ago pointed out, it was also a principal jumping off point for the experimental modernism of Frank Lloyd Wright. Remarkably, it was absorbed into popular building as a whole to become an important vernacular that flourished wherever Americans sought to depict themselves as the cultural inheritors of the English Colonial experience. For these reasons, *The Architecture of the American Summer: The Flowering of the Shingle Style* documents not only a particular architectural movement, but also an ongoing influence and ideal in American life.

The Architecture of the American Summer:
The Flowering of the Shingle Style

Introduction by Vincent Scully

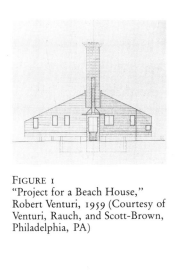

FIGURE 1
"Project for a Beach House,"
Robert Venturi, 1959 (Courtesy of
Venturi, Rauch, and Scott-Brown,
Philadelphia, PA)

It is good to see so many Shingle-Style designs together. They were a product of American culture's first long, warm summertime after the Civil War. Among them are a number of old friends long immured in the library stacks between the red, moldering covers of the *American Architect and Building News*. The demands of economy assigned a good many of them to the cutting room floor more than thirty years ago when my dissertation, *The Cottage Style*, of 1949, was being prepared for publication. Other periodicals, such as the dazzling *Architecture and Building*, no less than the *Inland Architect* and the *Western Architect*, have also been more extensively employed in this collection than they were before. The effect, on me at least, is of overpowering richness. The Shingle Style was clearly magisterial, pervasive, and national, and it lasted a long time: a point not sufficiently emphasized by me in 1949. So there are a great many designs illustrated here which were not included in the dissertation, in part because it came to a close when the architectural *avant garde* (if that term may be employed) of McKim, Mead and White, William Ralph Emerson, Peabody and Stearns, John Calvin Stevens, and so on, began to turn definitively against the Shingle Style after 1887. None of these architects ever did so entirely (Plate 87), but it is true that what might be called the most "innovative" years of the style as a "progressive" activity were past by the late eighties, though it is still not quite clear when the shingled mode as a whole came to an end. Perhaps, having entered into the mainstream of the American tradition of domestic building, it never really ended at all. There can be no doubt that it went into eclipse for a while—perhaps not before the First World War but surely by the time of the Second—and did not begin to revive until after the publication of *The Shingle Style* in 1955, with Robert Venturi's great Project for a Beach House, of 1959 (Fig. 1), sounding the first trumpet of its resurrection as a viable way of building in the present. I tried to analyze the early stages of that movement in *The Shingle Style Today*, of 1975. It has continued to gain strength to the present time and now figures prominently in a sustained revival of the vernacular and Classical traditions in general—a historical development which has occasioned the publication of this book.

The present revival calls into question the whole idea of *avant-garde* invention, as that phrase is used above. It also turns a skeptical eye on the hermetic and jealous concept of "style" as the Modern movement—or at least that aggressive wing of it which should be called the International style—had come to understand the word. My dissertation itself was written within a Modernist frame of reference. Though it set out to try to understand the nineteenth century on its own terms, it also regarded it as leading to something new, unique, and definite, as all Modernist historians have tried to make it do. So it tended to regard the traditional, Academic architecture of Beaux-Arts Classicism as the enemy and saw the Shingle Style as leading primarily to Frank Lloyd Wright—which it certainly did in part. But it did not stop there, and we might well argue that Wright's strictly disciplined, abstracted, iconoclastic way of designing—and after it that of the International Style— eventually proved more destructive of the Shingle Style than that of the Beaux-Arts had ever been.

The Shingle Style was in fact an integral part of the Colonial Revival. It was its liveliest manifestation, and it got along very well and for many years with the white-painted Classical details that characterized the Colonial Revival's later, more "Georgian," highly durable phase. All that, too, is part of the present revival, which the rigorous apologists of the Modern movement— perhaps myself a generation ago—would have condemned as an eclectic one. Indeed, some of the more intransigent Modernists still do so, objecting alike to this generation's renewed pleasure in decorative detail and to the vernacular and Classical traditions from which those details derived. Such critics are suspicious of the apparent freedom of choice exercised by the present revival, and, obsessed with "originality," they fail to value the fact that such choice is, in this case, rooted in and constrained and civilized by a concern for solid building types hardly susceptible to change. So the Shingle Style itself may seem at once visually lush and conceptually old-fashioned to minds shaped by the rigors of International-Style polemic, but there are more complicated issues involved.

Here a comparison should perhaps be drawn with Impressionist painting. Elsewhere I have noted its visual affinities with the Shingle Style, but the larger point might be a social one. Impressionism was middle-class painting *par excellence*. Its practitioners abandoned the overt social concerns of earlier nineteenth-century French painters in favor of overwhelming material sensation and the peace of the suburbs, perhaps not an especially admirable course of action in a social sense, but a fact, and one within which great painting was clearly possible at that time. And having embraced it, Impressionism has remained to this day the favorite painting of the middle class around the world; its exhibitions invariably outdraw everything else. The Shingle Style has much the same content and base. True enough, it can have a wonderful darkness in it, a rough animal presence and something wild of the mountains and the sea. Yet it is in the end an architecture of suburban relaxation and country joys. It reflects an American middle class grown rich after the Civil War, prepared to enjoy itself, and, despite the nostalgic yearning toward Colonial simplicity and a smaller, cleaner America which helped give the style birth, it is in the end as gently warm and sheltering as the well-intentioned middle-class families who built it. Its renewed success in the late twentieth century taps and expresses a similar social source and reflects a comparable historical moment. There is a lot of money around but almost no governmental assistance for low-cost housing and not much return for developers in economical building. Hence the present phase of the Shingle Style is not normally creating the common buildings for which it is ideally suited but expensive private houses and condominiums instead. An *arriére garde* of Modernist critics therefore tends to oppose the present movement on visual and social grounds alike, much as their precursors among the early abstract artists and critics despised Impressionism. It seems too simply hedonistic to them, and, like Impressionist painting, the drawings in this collection can be taken as shameless examples of that. They are physically rich, exploring every material and surface with loving care, filling our eyes with warm, spreading forms. They are objects of delight, full of confidence in their powers, and they aim to please.

It is somewhat embarrassing to me at this time to reread the stern lines I wrote almost forty years ago about the Shingle Style's movement toward "order" and "unity." There was of course such a movement, and it eventually shaped the powerful forms that are so well represented in the later drawings of this collection. But the style had another important aspect too: its generous capacity for play. Architects of the 1960s, such as Venturi and Charles Moore, recognized that quality and identified it as a fundamentally liberating force— from, in particular, the humorless reductionism of the International Style. They grasped the fact that ambiguity and its concomitant "Mannerism" shaped the very heart of the Modern experience at its freest and most true, and they saw that the Shingle Style combined reasonable contemporary programs and structure with real freedom in detail—with, in other words, Sir Henry Wotton's "Delight." They, and now thousands of young architects after them, have therefore been released from the confines of a polemically "Modern" style to the richer contextualities which have normally characterized architecture and which are, indeed, especially reasonable in the pluralism of the Modern period.

3

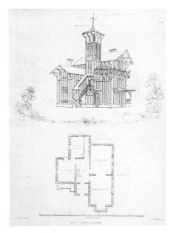

FIGURE 2
"A Perspective View of a Cottage in the Swiss Style," Plate XLVI, Brooks, S.H., *Designs for Cottage and Villa Architecture*, London: Thomas Kelly, Pasternoster Row. (AIA Archives)

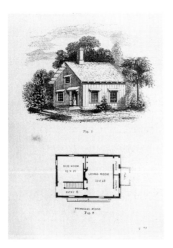

FIGURE 3
"A Labourer's Cottage," Design I, Fig. 5, Downing, Andrew Jackson, *The Architecture of Country Houses*, New York: Dover Publications, 1969. (AIA Archives)

It is clear, nevertheless, that the delightful drawings in this book were made by architects (and what were called "delineators" at the time) who were all working in a style. Anything so clear-cut deserves a name. It cannot satisfactorily be called either "Queen Anne" or "Colonial," although both those terms were often applied to it interchangeably during its period. In fact, like so many fundamental bodies of work in the history of art, the Shingle Style came to be so taken for granted as the way to do things that it never really had a name of its own during its early years, by which I mean the period treated in this book. I therefore make no apologies for having ventured to name it as I did. The name helped it to be recognized by those who had lost it, and it is at least more directly descriptive than many similar historical identifications such as "Cubism," "Gothic," and "Baroque" have ever been.

We ask ourselves further what the distinguishing characteristics of the style seem to be as they are exhibited in this representative collection. It is worth trying to answer that question briefly from today's perspective, without attempting to repeat the entire argument of the book. The first characteristic, underlying all others as an almost unconscious substructure, is a common confidence in vernacular wood-frame construction. That confidence has to be regarded as a legacy from the Stick Style—for whose name again no apology is tendered—of the period circa 1840–1876. An argument may indeed be made for the fact that the Stick Style was distinguished from its European cousins by its more total obsession with wood-frame construction as the major generator of visual effects, though these were, of course, fundamentally Picturesque and so international in character. Indeed, English Picturesque prototypes, of the kind popularized by J.C. Loudon and others, first brought the wooden skeleton to the surface (Fig. 2), dominated by the vertical post, and from that moment everything happened very rapidly and with a special social and technological freshness in America. Andrew Jackson Downing and a horde of builders of single-family houses from Maine to California could even achieve the new effects in small buildings with vertical planks and battens alone, without employing vertical studs at all (Fig. 3). When vertical boards and battens were used to sheathe the more usual skeleton frames, diagonal braces, serving as nailers, were set in across the studs (Fig. 4). This was especially necessary in the new balloon-frame construction invented in America, where the joists, at least theoretically, rose continuously upward past all the horizontal members of the frame, which might otherwise have served as nailers for the siding themselves. Clearly, however, Downing and the others admired the multiplied verticals of the balloon frame and sought to achieve that effect in its sheathing, as Fig. 4 (which was in my dissertation but cut from the book) abundantly shows. So the early Stick Style, with its battens and skeletal porches, took form (Fig. 5). Soon, however, the diagonal braces became of

FIG. 107.— *Isometrical Perspective View of the Balloon Frame.*

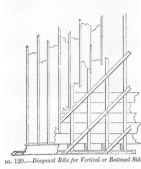

IG. 120.—*Diagonal Ribs for Vertical or Battened Sid*

FIG. 113.—*Isometrical Perspective Balloon Frame.*

FIGURE 4
Figures 107, 113, 120, Woodward, George E., *Woodward's Country Homes*, New York: Geo. E. Woodward, 1865. (AIA Archives)

FIGURE 5
Board and Batten House, Newport, RI.

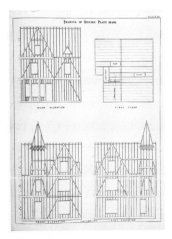

FIGURE 6
Plate 64, Bicknell, Amos J., *Bicknell's Cottage and Villa Architecture*. New York: A.J. Bicknell & Co., Architectural Book Publishers, 1878. (AIA Archives)

special interest in themselves. They were capable of achieving more complicated and dynamic effects, which I called "baroque" when I first wrote about them (Fig. 6 & Plate 3), and which were indeed representative of the fully developed stage of Picturesque design as an international movement. Nevertheless, the Stick Style tradition tended in general to produce much simpler work, of which a house of 1876 by William Ralph Emerson, published in *The Architectural Sketchbook* in that year, is an excellent example (Plate 4). Emerson was to become one of the most skilful of practitioners of the Shingle Style, but the Stick Style provided the framework upon which it was all to be hung, that of vernacular wood construction.

The Shingle-Style architects, as the first self-conscious generation of professional architects in the United States, set out to enliven that vernacular tradition in certain quite specific ways. First, beginning with H. H. Richardson in 1874, came the new openness, liveliness, and ingenuity in plan which was to characterize the Shingle Style throughout its history. The domestic program had never before produced such a flexible and varied set of schemes for living spaces, and that inventiveness was brought into three dimensions through an equal flexibility of approach to section and massing. Though I used the word "organic" more easily forty years ago than I would today, there is nevertheless a marvelously life-like connection between plan, section, and massing in Shingle-Style buildings. It was not a strict, wholly "integrated," machined connection like that worked out by Frank Lloyd Wright—one which bound the "organism" within its dominant rhythms—but a flexible and liberating one, possibly closer to the complexities of living organisms than the later, more abstract systems of Modern architecture were. Finally came the shingled surface, from which the name was derived. This was a true skin, covering up the old, actually or symbolically exposed, frame of the Stick Style and subordinating the inner structure of the building to a whole range of surface effects free of structure. Out of this opportunity, or instigating it, a varied repertory of decorative details arose—from fancifully cut shingles to plaster panels, mullioned windows, sunflowers, scrolls, screens, and, eventually, gleaming white columns, pediments, and dentilled cornices. Visually intoxicating as they were, most of those details were also alive with an intensely symbolic content, asking to be recognized as culturally charged quotations and referring generally to identification alike with the Colonial past and with the new English "Aesthetic" taste. The shingles were normally dark, the details at first equally so, later much lighter, finally glowing in white paint against the shadowy masses of the building. So the houses were both new and old, freely serving and suggesting every kind of domestic relaxation while at the same time linking modern life with an American past seemingly more primordial than it had ever been in fact and endowed with a national history freshly valued and newly loved. It all added up to an eloquent architectural language, free and easy but with its depths, at once rational enough and endlessly resourceful in fancy.

It is wonderful to watch that language developing through the years, especially to see it through the eyes of E. Eldon Deane (Plate 36), the demon renderer of the period. Deane's sketches come out crawling with life in the photo-lithographic reproductions of the new *American Architect and Building News*, founded in 1876 and the major disseminating agent of the Shingle Style, and they have now once again become models for draftsmen in some contemporary architectural offices, if perhaps not yet in schools. Certainly all the drawings in the *American Architect and Building News* look even better now than they did forty years ago, and some that were not especially noticed before come to prominence. One by Thomas Hastings, published in 1879, is a good example of that (Plate 9). Hastings is heard of very little thereafter until he emerges as an important figure in Beaux-Arts Classicism, but this drawing is a couple of years ahead of its time in plan and elevation alike. It must have had a decided effect on Wilson Eyre, who brought a more decisive tension to the plan but never outdid Hastings' brilliantly fenestrated exterior.

The smallest houses of all also have a special appeal today, when they can be taken as models in ways we were not prepared to explore forty years ago. A little project by John A. Fox, not an overly prominent architect, suggests designs by Venturi (Plate 14). If Fox is being candid about the date of 1872, his building transcends its Stick-Style moment; though a bit awkward in plan, it is a timeless little structure otherwise. There are many others. Henry Paston Clark's "Small Summer House" for Kennebunkport seems no less delightful than it did a generation ago, but it offers more direct suggestions for new building as well (Plate 15). Everything looks more timely now; the generations syncopate. (The historical crevasse that Modernism created is closing.) Clark's compact but expansive Sprague House is no slouch either (Plate 26). It is a precursor of the massing type that Bruce Price was to Mayanize into monu-

FIGURE 7
House and Studio by and for
Frank Lloyd Wright, Oak Park,
IL, 1889. (Archives of Henry-
Russell Hitchcock, courtesy of
Mosette Broderick)

mentality at Tuxedo Park to catch, all unknowing, Frank Lloyd Wright's young eye (Plate 54 & Fig. 7). Dabney's "Redcote" (Plate 24) seems to cap the lot at the moment, with its impeccably reasonable plan and eloquently varied windows, one with an outrageous pediment. The huge posts of the porch apparently bothered me a bit years ago but, as the work of Venturi has since shown us, they look absolutely right to set off at once the tiny scale of the whole building and the big scale of the pedimented window. And how well the thick-mullioned windows hold the surface; how telling when one, however small, is opened. What a building it is. Can it still be there? Was it, indeed, ever built? If not, someone will probably build it sooner or later.

In this essential, Mannerist vein, Stanford White is still immortal. His Casino at Short Hills is one of the pure delights, pushing out a shell pediment under its big gable and setting a wing to the tower (Plate 27). How tragic that it burned. All the more Classically detailed work of White and his partners—pseudo-Georgian, play-Palladian, adulterated Adam, or whatever it should be called—looks better and better today, more than ever sparkling with exuberance and wit as our eyes are progressively freed from prejudice to see it (Plate 30). At the same time, a competition in the *American Architect and Building News* of 1885 for "A Small Stable to Cost $1500" catches our eyes now, as it apparently did not catch mine before. Here is a program exactly tailored to that love of the picturesque which most of these architects shared (Plates 38 & 41). It is also very close to the normally modest programs of vernacular building—small in scale, economical, and great fun.

A running "Competition for a $5000 House" comes along in 1886. Not much sign of lassitude in the Shingle Style there. A few of the designs are as outrageous as some of their descendants of the 1980s (Plates 48–49). Others are triumphs of compaction (Plate 50). Most use a lot of rooms and convey a timeless impression of pushing the budget.

There are rather more shingled churches for suburbs and summer resorts among the drawings than one might have expected (Plate 17). Their few, large, and simple forms tend to be drawn by the continuous shingle surface into unusually compact and powerful masses. Their religion, as contrasted with that housed in the taut, clapboarded, white-painted churches of the Colonial tradition, would seem an earthy one, pretending at least to celebrate that protective and benevolent Nature which their parishioners, in fact, had come to adore. Even more striking is the steadily increasing number of designs for country hotels. There are a few in the seventies, among them a Stick-Style barn at Bar Harbor by Bruce Price (Plate 7), but they really get going in the eighties, with the return of a more general prosperity coinciding with the heyday of the Shingle Style itself. The series amply demonstrates how powerful that style could be in larger buildings, and it continues to gain in monumental breadth as the late eighties are left behind. The forms become ever more voluminous, swelling with expansive interior spaces and extending horizontally out to continuous porches (Plate 72). One of the earlier among them is a project for Los Angeles (Plate 33), and the series culminates with photographs (new to the *American Architect*) of a grand complex of 1890 with a science-fiction tower (Plate 122). Country clubs, too, however smug in program, produce forms of comparable power, though generally at somewhat smaller scale (Plates 29, 82, 93, 172).

The monumentality so strikingly embodied in the hotels and the clubs is characteristic of the general development of the Shingle Style as a whole in the years directly after 1887 (Plate 62), and it produced a surprising number of public buildings, especially hospitals and libraries, which demonstrated a unique combination of sculptural power and public presence with a marvelously qualified domestic scale (Plates 105, 147, 166). The frontal gable had always been a key feature in the monumentality of the Shingle Style. It culminated in 1887, in McKim, Mead and White's incomparable Low House at Bristol, Rhode Island (Plate 59), one vast triangular shape upon which Venturi's Project of 1959 was to be based (Fig. 1). The frontal gable had of course been employed as a dominant element by Richardson in the Watts-Sherman House of 1874 (Plate 1), at the very beginning of the whole business, and it hangs on as such during the nineties, even while the Shingle Style is progressively losing its monopoly on domestic design (Plates 145, 149). As it wanes, it tends to become either bigger or more quirky—noticeably so at Tuxedo where the original modest "Honeymoon cottages" by Price, so essential alike to Wright in the late eighties and to the renewed Shingle Style of the present, are blown up in scale or burlesqued in the later buildings there (Plates 53, 54, 55, 118, 145, 179).

It is interesting to see what happens to the stars of the eighties in later years. Wilson Eyre, for example, seems to try to use more masonry and less wood and so tends to look more and more European (Plate 133). His plans, too, become rather more compartmentalized, with their halls treated more purely as elements of circulation rather than as rooms to live in (Plate 135). Architects better known for other types of buildings, such as the skyscraper, also swim into orbit. When they do so they seem to base their work on that of the more specialized Shingle Style practitioners, as L.S. Buffington does on McKim, Mead and White, Lamb and Rich, and John Calvin Stevens (Plate 89). The future luminaries of the Beaux-Arts—like Hastings, mentioned earlier— also make brief Shingle Style appearances in their early domestic work, with Horace Trumbauer, Bertram Goodhue, and Claude Bragdon among them (Plates 9, 69, 103, 134). In 1899 the *American Architect* published the spectacular Foster mansion by Carrère and Hastings. It is wholly Classical in plan

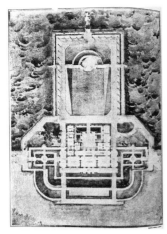

(Fig. 8) and stretches out to a fine, formal, and appropriately haunting Italian garden, like those being explored by Edith Wharton and her friends during those years (Fig. 9). The house itself is a more or less French, early Renaissance type, influenced by Serlio and others, and it rather eerily resembles a good deal of the more elaborately "Post-Modern" work being done at the present time (Fig. 10). We sense that the Classical elements are graphically conceived and not quite under control, but they are obviously a delight to the designer and are therefore still involved in some of the playful vitality of the Shingle Style itself.

Perhaps the most important new evidence presented by this collection of drawings is of the Shingle Style's geographical spread. It is to be found literally throughout the country, but it seems, significantly enough, to have been strongest on both coasts and in Chicago—in those areas, in fact, where the most important and the liveliest new work of the early twentieth century came to be done. Its associational factor—its evocation of the Colonial past—must have worked powerfully for it far off on the prairie and among the palms. Nevertheless, from the Middle West to San Francisco and Los Angeles, its early practitioners were soon inspired by it to more regional, more "original" styles of their own (Plates 32, 34, 37, 79, 110, 176, 199, 214).

The nineties, when the Shingle Style was beginning to dwindle in the East, was the great decade of its national efflorescence. A whole series of houses in California by a number of different architects is published as photographs in the *American Architect* and the *Western Architect* during these years and later. In some of them we can see McKim, Mead and White turning into Greene and Greene before our eyes (Plate 177). Schweinfurth's First Unitarian Church at Berkeley, of 1898, even makes a direct leap from the Shingle Style of the 1880s to that of the present time. The big circular window it introduces into the Low House's frontal gable has become a stock-in-trade of contemporary work. In California itself, the Shingle Style formed the matrix from which the region's own lively modern vernacular in wood was to develop, balancing a complementary masonry tradition of Spanish Colonial derivation.

Back home, on the East Coast, many of the older Shingle Style architects continued to work on into the new century, joined by younger Classicists such as John Russell Pope in their more relaxed vacation houses. W. A. Bates, whose work in several geographical areas appears in the *American Architect* from its earliest days but who somehow never quite seems to make the front rank, nevertheless proves his own personal durability, and Shingle-Style houses by him back in Bronxville, strongly Richardsonian if a little shaggy in character, are published as photographs in 1900 (Plate 192). There are many other little-known, more or less parochial architects who performed excellently well in this idiom, among them E. G. W. Dietrich and I. H. Green, who did a good deal of work on Long Island. This is of course the fundamental character of a

FIGURE 12
"H.A.C. Taylor House," McKim, Mead and White, 1885–86, Sheldon, George William (ed.), *Artistic Country-Seats, Vol. II, Types of Recent American Villa and Cottage Architecture (with instances of Country Club Houses)*; New York: Da Capo Press, 1979 (unabridged reprint of v. 1–2, 1886 edition published by D. Appleton & Co., New York), p. 8. (AIA Archives)

FIGURE 11
Harold C. Bradley House, [Woods Hole, MA], Purcell and Elmslie, 1911–12. (Sandak, Inc.)

reasonable tradition: that almost everyone can do acceptable work within it (Plates 64, 113). The rich body of shingled houses at Southampton on Long Island, dating from early—and late—in the twentieth century, is a case in point.

Finally, the Shingle Style continued to affect the work of many of the architects of the Prairie School long after Wright himself had designed it away. Purcell and Elmslie's Bradley House, taking off like an airplane across the Sound at Wood's Hole, is the most striking of many such examples (Fig. 11). It combines Wright's early Winslow and his transcendent Robie houses and swathes the amalgam in shingles once again. Despite all that, however, it was the Classical tradition which shaped most of the new work of the early years of the century. In 1900, a wonderfully overscaled pastiche by Ludlow and Valentine after the H.A.C. Taylor House, in which McKim, Mead and White first began to set their faces toward Classicizing design, made its appearance (Fig. 12 & Plate 189). It was in fact only one of the many reflections, copies, and adaptions of the H.A.C. Taylor House that are to be found pretty much all over the United States. The Georgian (really Adamesque) type that McKim, Mead and White hit upon there apparently turned out to be the archetypal one; it, too, demonstrated its durability as the years went on.

The Shingle Style itself continued to be widely published, if in dwindling numbers, until the First World War, and scattered examples of it, some of them

FIGURE 13
"House in Minneapolis, Minn.,"
Harry W. Jones, *The American
Architect*, Vol. 98, No. 1817; Oct.
19, 1910. (Avery Library, Colum-
bia University)

quite distinguished, appeared in architectural magazines as late as the 1920s
(Plate 227). After that, as was suggested earlier, it did not, I think, so much die
out as, in dwindled, impoverished form, slide below the conscious interest of
the profession into the general mass of vernacular building. But before that
happened, the Shingle Style had already tended either toward the more simply
Colonial (Plate 211) or back toward the "Jacobethan" English from which it
had also derived in the alchemy of its beginning (Fig. 12). So it all seems to
break up into its original components toward the last, but persistent echoes of
its life-giving plans continue to appear in it, often awkward, heavy-handed,
and out of scale, awaiting regeneration in a new day.

Abbreviations of illustration sources:
AIA Archives: American Institute of Architects Archives
AIC: Art Institute of Chicago, Ryerson and Burnham Libraries

PLATE 1
"Cottage at Newport for
William Watts Sherman,"
Gambrill and Richardson,
*New York Sketchbook of
Architecture*, Vol. 2, No. 5,
May 1875. (AIA Archives)

PLATE 2
"Residence of T. G. Ap-
pleton at Newport, [RI],"
Richard Morris Hunt, F.M.
Howe, del.; *American Ar-
chitect and Building News*,
Vol. 1, No. 1, Jan. 1, 1876.
(AIA Archives)

13

New Jersey Headquarters · Centennial International Exhibition · 1876 ·

PLATE 4
"House built for the Misses
Forbes [Milton, MA, near
Mattapan]," William Ralph
Emerson, B.A. Rich, del.;
*The Architectural Sketch-
book*, Vol. 3, No. 10, April
1876. (AIA Archives)

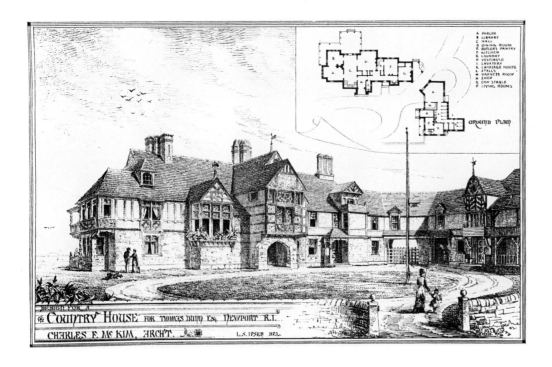

PLATE 5
"Country House for
Thomas Nunn [Newport,
RI]," Charles McKim, L.S.
Ipsen, del.; *American Ar-
chitect and Building News*,
Vol. 2, No. 83, July 28,
1877. (AIA Archives)

PLATE 6
"Bird's Eye View of House
for James Cheney [South
Manchester, CT],"
Gambrill and Richardson,
*American Architecture and
Building News*, Vol. 3, No.
126, May 25, 1878. (AIA
Archives)

Plan of
Principal Floor

·Bird's·Eye·View·of·House·

Cheney · Eꜱǫ · · South · Manchester · Conn · ∴ · Gambrill & Richardson · Arch'ts

PLATE 7
"West End Hotel [Bar Harbor, Mt. Desert, ME]," Bruce Price, *American Architect and Building News*, Vol. 5, No. 161, Jan. 25, 1879. (AIA Archives)

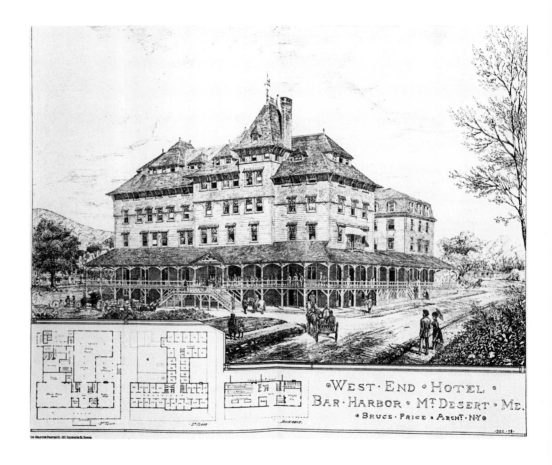

PLATE 8
"House at Mt. Desert, ME," William Ralph Emerson, B.A. Rich, del.; *American Architect and Building News*, Vol. 5, No. 169, March 22, 1879. (AIA Archives)

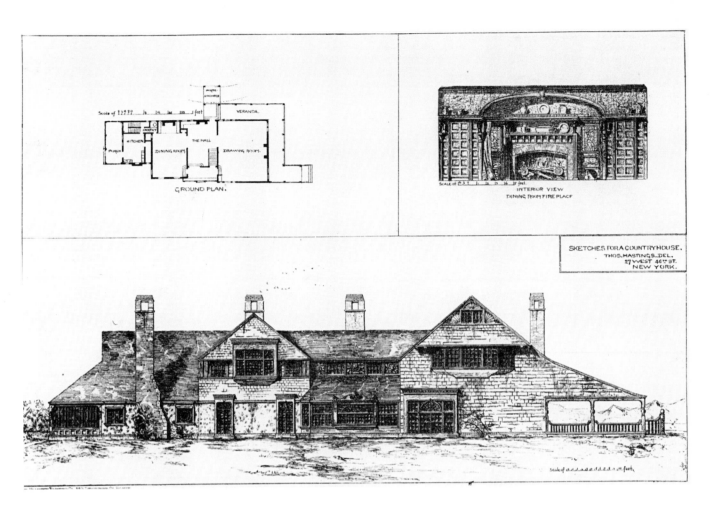

GROUND PLAN.

INTERIOR VIEW
DINING ROOM FIRE PLACE

SKETCHES FOR A COUNTRY HOUSE.
THOS. HASTINGS. DEL.
27 WEST 46TH ST.
NEW YORK.

PLATE 9
"Sketches for a Country
House," Thomas Hastings,
*American Architect and
Building News*, Vol. 6, No.
200, Oct. 25, 1879. (AIA
Archives)

House·for·Mrs·A·C·Alden ~ on·Fort·Hill·
Lloyds·Neck··Long·Island·
Mc·Kim·Mead·&·Bigelow·Architects·57·Broadway·New·York

THE HELIOTYPE PRINTING CO. 220 DEVONSHIRE ST BOSTON

PLATE 10
"House for Mrs. A. C. Alden on Fort Hill [Lloyd's Neck, LI]," McKim, Mead and Bigelow, *American Architect and Building News*, Vol. 6, No. 192, Aug. 30, 1879. (AIA Archives)

PLATE 11
"Sketch for 'the Craigs'
[Mt. Desert, ME]," Bruce
Price, *American Architect
and Building News*, Vol. 6,
No. 209, Dec. 27, 1879.
(AIA Archives)

PLATE 11
Sketch for 'the Craigs'

PLATE 14
"A Parallel of Low Cost
Country Houses: A House
at Downer Landing, MA,
built in 1872, Cost
$1,500," John A. Fox,
*American Architect and
Building News*, Vol. 8, No.
236, July 3, 1880. (AIA
Archives)

View.

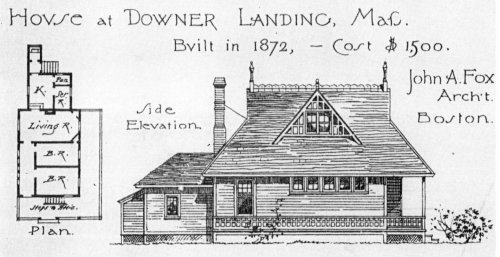

House at DOWNER LANDING, Mass.

Built in 1872, — Cost $1500.

John A. Fox
Arch't.
Boston.

Side
Elevation.

Plan.

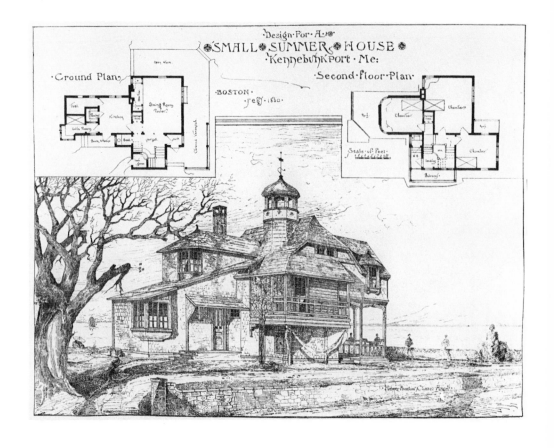

PLATE 17
"Church of St. Sylvia
[Mount Desert, ME],"
William Ralph Emerson,
*American Architect and
Building News*, Vol. 9, No.
287, June 25, 1881. (AIA
Archives)

PLATE 18
"House at Beverly Farms,"
William Ralph Emerson,
A.W. Cobb, del.; *American
Architect and Building
News*, Vol. 9, No. 287,
June 25, 1881. (AIA
Archives)

LAMB & RICH ARCHTS
346-348 BROADWAY N.Y.

Residence of Robert Seney
Bernardsville N.J.

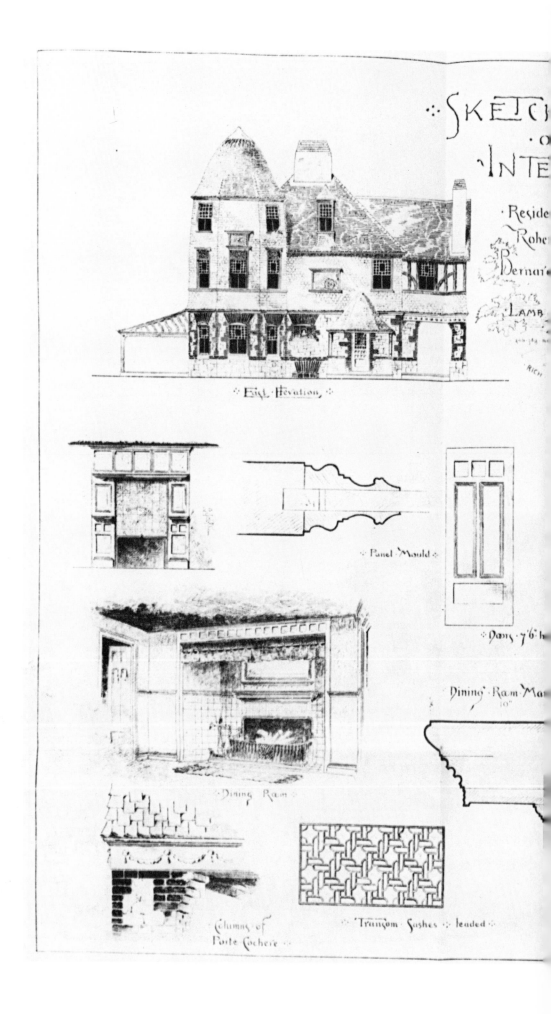

Porte·Cochère·Entrance

Dining·Mantle

Conductor

Architrave

Hall·Mantle
Stone·and·Brick

Hall·Shelf

Rail

Hall Balustrade of Wicker·work

Hall·to·Dining·Rm

HALL
Wall·of·Hand·Floated·Plaster

PLATE 21
"Cottage at Short Hills
Park, NJ," Lamb and Rich,
*American Architect and
Building News*, Vol. 10,
No. 315, Jan. 7, 1882.
(AIA Archives)

Design for
Country Hotel Barn.
By "Jockey".

A. Page Brown.

PLATE 22
"Design for a Country
Hotel Barn by 'Jockey,'"
A. Page Brown, *American
Architect and Building
News*, Vol. 12, No. 341,
July 8, 1882. (AIA Archives)

PLATE 23
"Grasshead House,
[Swampscott, MA],"
Arthur Little, *American
Architect and Building
News*, Vol. 12, No. 347,
Aug. 19, 1882. (AIA
Archives)

PLATE 24
"Redcote, [York Harbor,
ME]," William Dabney,
*American Architect and
Building News*, Vol. 12,
No. 351, Sept. 16, 1882.
(AIA Archives)

· FIRST FLOOR PLAN ·

PLATE 25
"Cottage near Short Hills,
NJ," William A. Bates,
*American Architect and
Building News*, Vol. 12,
No. 350, Sept. 9, 1882.
(AIA Archives)

PLATE 28
"A Cottage to Cost about $3000," A.W. Cobb, *American Architect and Building News*, Vol. 13, No. 377, March 17, 1883. (AIA Archives)

PLATE 29
"Washington Park Club House [Chicago, IL]," S. S. Beman, *Inland Architect*, Vol. 1, No. 6, July 1883. (AIC)

PLATE 30
"Miss Julia Appleton's
House [Lenox, MA],"
McKim, Mead and White,
1883–84, Sheldon, George
William (ed.), *Artistic
Country-Seats, Vol. I, Types
of Recent American Villa
and Cottage Architecture
(with instances of Country
Club Houses)*; New York:
Da Capo Press, 1979 (un-
abridged reprint of v. 1–2,
1886 edition published by
D. Appleton & Co., New
York, p. 61. (AIA
Archives)

PLATE 31
"Sunset Hall, Residence of
Mr. S. P. Hinckley [Law-
rence, LI]," Lamb and
Rich, Rich, del.; *American
Architect and Building
News*, Vol. 15, No. 425,
Feb. 2, 1884. (AIA
Archives)

Geo. D. Rainsford
Wm. A. Bates. Archts.
149 Bway.
New York.

Library
11x13

Hall
16x19

Kitchen
13x19

P.

Dining Room
15x17

Pantry

piazza

GROUND PLAN

PLATE 32
"House in Cheyenne City,
Wyoming Territory, for
Mr. William Sturgis Jr.,"
George D. Rainsford and
William A. Bates, *American Architect and Building
News*, Vol. 15, No. 435,
April 26, 1884. (AIA
Archives)

Proposed Hotel
at
Los Angelos
California

Franz E. Zerrahn
Architect 68 Devonshire St.
Boston, Mass.

PLATE 33
"Proposed Hotel, Los Angeles, CA" Franz E. Zerrahn, *American Architect
and Building News*, Vol.
15, No. 436, May 3, 1884.
(AIA Archives)

PLATE 34
"House of J.A. Ammon
[Cleveland, OH]," J.A.
Schweinfurth, *American
Architect and Building
News*, Vol. 16, No. 459,
Oct. 11, 1884. (AIA
Archives)

PLATE 35
"House at Portland, ME,
for John Calvin Stevens,"
*American Architect and
Building News*, Vol. 16,
No. 469, Dec. 20, 1884.
(AIA Archives)

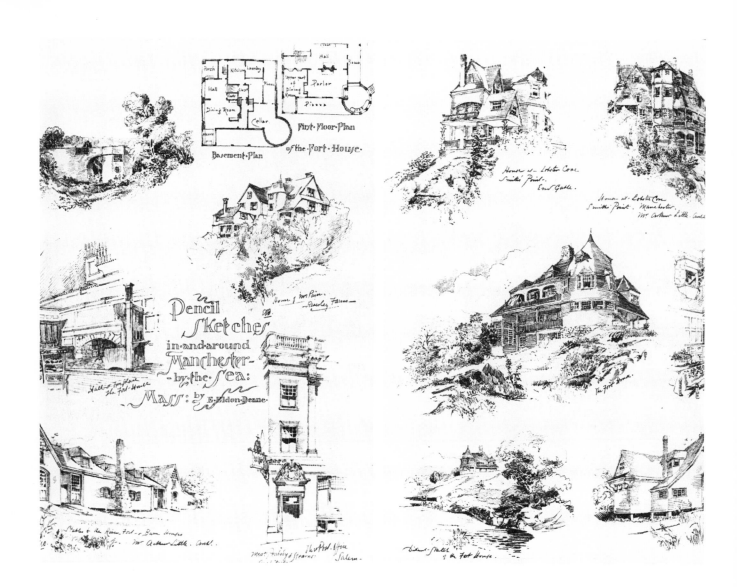

PLATE 36
"Pencil Sketches in and around Manchester-by-the-Sea, MA, by E. Eldon Deane" *American Architect and Building News*, Vol. 17, No. 472, Jan. 10, 1885. (AIA Archives)

HOUSE in CHEYENNE, WY.

William A. Bates and Geo. D. Rainsford, Archts. 119 Bway, New York.

PLATE 37
"House in Cheyenne,
WY," William A. Bates and
George D. Rainsford,
*American Architect and
Building News*, Vol. 17,
No. 476, Feb. 7, 1885.
(AIA Archives)

PLATE 38
"Small Stable to cost
$1500," Frank E. Wallis,
*American Architect and
Building News*, Vol. 17,
No. 478, Feb. 21, 1885.
(AIA Archives)

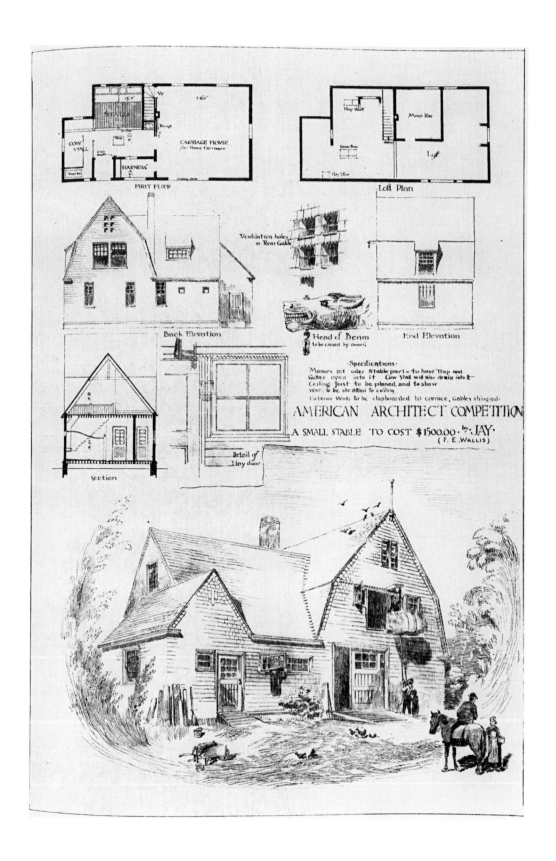

PLATE 39
"Montezuma Hotel [Las Vegas, NM]," Burnham and Root, Paul C. Lantrup, del., *Inland Architect and Builder*, Vol. 5, No. 3, April 1885. (AIA Archives)

Library & Boudoir.

Interior of Hall.

Roof & Beam of Gable.

er by the sea

From the Drive.

Sketch in the Vicinity.

PLATE 41
"Stable for $1000–1500, by
'Hostler,'" *American Ar-
chitect and Building News*,
Vol. 17, No. 480, March 7,
1885. (AIA Archives)

COPYRIGHTED, 1886, TICKNOR & CO.

Picturesque Bits at Cushings'

THE THAXTER COTTAGE

"Dakers"

THE FARM BUILDINGS

THE FARM HOUSE

JOHN CALVIN STEVENS
ARCHITECT
PORTLAND. ME.
1ST. NAT. BANK BLDG.

AT THE OTTAWA.

PLATE 42
"Picturesque Bits at Cushings," John Calvin Stevens, *American Architect and Building News*, Vol. 19, No. 527, Jan. 30, 1886. (AIA Archives)

PLATE 43
"Gate Lodge for Mr.
Flagler [Mamaroneck,
NY]," H.J. Hardenburgh.
Architecture and Building,
Vol. 4, No. 7, Feb. 13,
1886. (AIC)

PLATE 44
"Coachman's Cottage for
Mr. W.P. Tuckerman
[Chester Bay, LI],"
McKim, Mead and White,
Architecture and Building,
Vol. 4, No. 7, Feb. 13,
1886. (AIC)

PLATE 45
"Sketch for a House at
Interlaken, FL," E. M.
Wheelwright, *American
Architect and Building
News*, Vol. 19, No. 530,
Feb. 20, 1886. (AIA
Archives)

· DESIGN·FOR·CITY·RESIDENCES ·
· Hodgson · and · Stem · Archts · St · Paul · Minn ·

PLATE 46
"Design for City Resi-
dences," Hodgson and
Stem, *Architecture and
Building*, Vol. 4, No. 13,
March 27, 1886 (AIA
Archives)

PLATE 47
"Sketch for a Mountain
House," Andrews and
Jacques, *American Architect
and Building News*, Vol.
19, No. 543, May 22, 1886.
(AIA Archives)

PLATE 48
"A $5000 House by
'Charles Dickens,'"
Edward F. Maher, *American Architect and Building
News*, Vol. 20, No. 551,
July 17, 1886. (AIA
Archives)

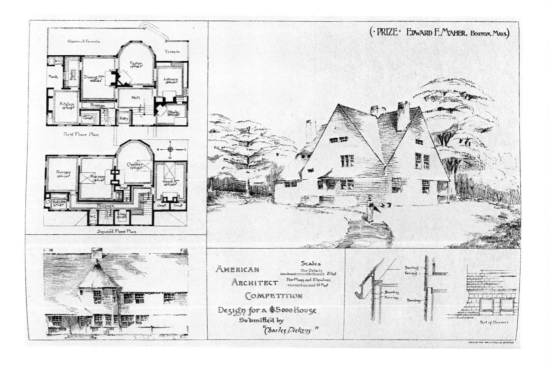

First Floor Plan

Second Floor Plan

Attic Plan

A $5000 House
American Architect Competition
Submitted by "W"

Rear Elevation

Entrance Door

Detail of Front Porch

Rake Moulding

Water Table

Window Jamb

View in Hall

Detail of Stairs

Elevation of Dormer

Heliotype Printing Co. Boston

PLATE 49
"A $5000 House by 'W,'"
*American Architect and
Building News*, Vol. 20,
No. 554, Aug. 7, 1886.
(AIA Archives)

PLATE 50
"Novelist's Home, by 'In-
connu,' " *American Architect and Building News*,
Vol. 20, No. 556, Aug. 2.,
1886. (AIA Archives)

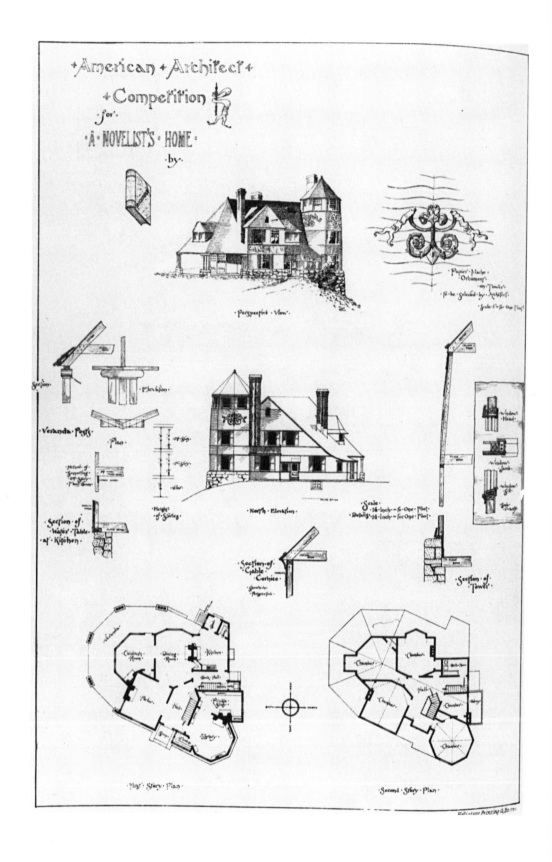

PLATE 51
"House of Lyman C.
Josephs [Newport, RI],"
C.S. Luce, E. Eldon De-
ane, del.; *American Archi-
tect and Building News*,
Vol. 20, No. 556, Aug. 21,
1886. (AIA Archives)

PLATE 52
"Tower Hill Cottage [Tux-
edo Park, NY]," Bruce
Price, *Architecture and
Building*, Vol. 5, No. 10,
Sept. 4, 1886. (AIC)

PLATE 53
"A Cottage at Tuxedo
Park," Bruce Price, *Archi-
tecture and Building*, Vol.
5, No. 11, Sept. 11, 1886.
(AIC)

A Cottage - Tuxedo Park.
New Jersey.
Bruce Price. Architect.

Fred Wright del.

PLATE 54
"A Cottage at Tuxedo Park," Bruce Price, *Architecture and Building*, Vol. 5, No. 12, Sept. 18, 1886. (AIC)

A Cottage - Tuxedo Park.

Bruce Price. Architect.

Fred Wright del.

PLATE 55
"A Cottage at Tuxedo Park," Bruce Price, *Architecture and Building*, Vol. 5, No. 13, Sept. 25, 1886. (AIC)

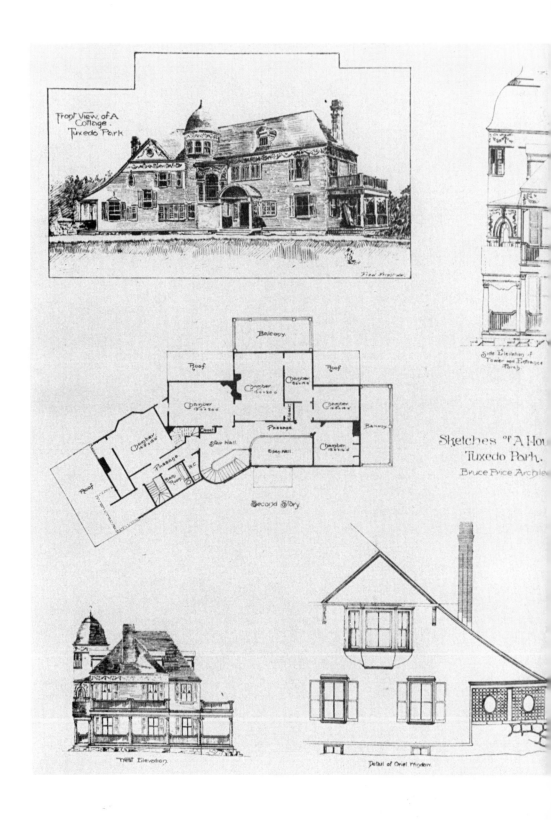

Front View of A Cottage. Tuxedo Park

Side Elevation of Tower and Entrance Porch

Sketches of A House Tuxedo Park.

Bruce Price Architect

Balcony.

Roof

Chamber

Chamber

Chamber

Roof

Chamber

Passage

Balcony

Stair Hall

Open Hall

Chamber

Chamber

Passage

Bath Room

W.C.

Roof

Second Story

West Elevation

Detail of Oriel Window.

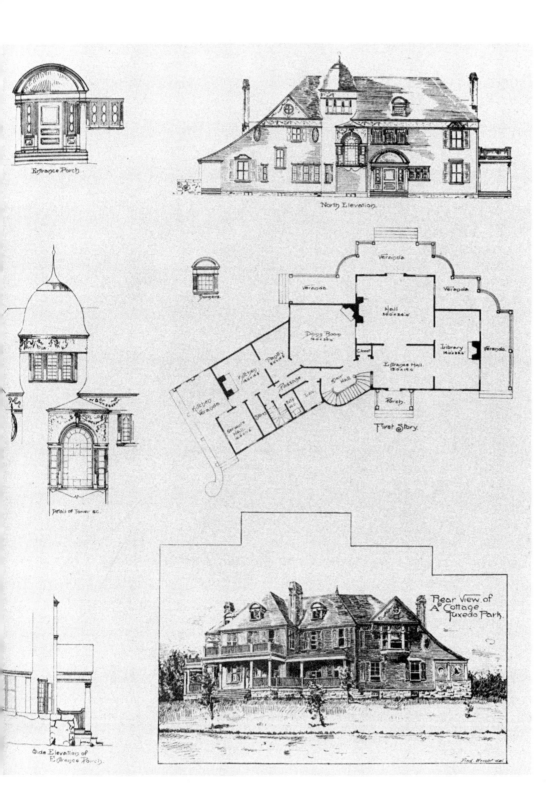

Entrance Porch.

North Elevation.

Details of Tower &c.

First Story.

Rear View of A Cottage Tuxedo Park.

Side Elevation of Entrance Porch.

PLATE 56
"Sketches of a House at Tuxedo Park," Bruce Price, *Architecture and Building*, Vol. 5, No. 14, Oct. 2, 1886. (AIC)

PLATE 57
"A House by the Sea,"
John Calvin Stevens, *Architecture and Building*, Vol. 5, No. 18, Oct. 30, 1886. (AIC)

PLATE 58
"House built near Quogue, LI," William A. Bates, *American Architect and Building News*, Vol. 20, No. 572, Dec. 11, 1886. (AIA Archives)

PLATE 59
William G. Low House,
Bristol, RI, 1886–87;
McKim, Mead and White.
(Courtesy of Richard
Longstreth)

PLATE 60
"House for C.A. Potter
[Chestnut Hill, PA]," *Ar-
chitecture and Building,*
Vol. 5, No. 26, Dec. 25,
1886. (AIA Archives)

PLATE 61
"Stations on the Boston
and Albany Railroad,"
H.H. Richardson, sketched
by E. Eldon Deane, *American Architect and Building
News*, Vol. 21, No. 583,
Feb. 26, 1887. (AIA
Archives)

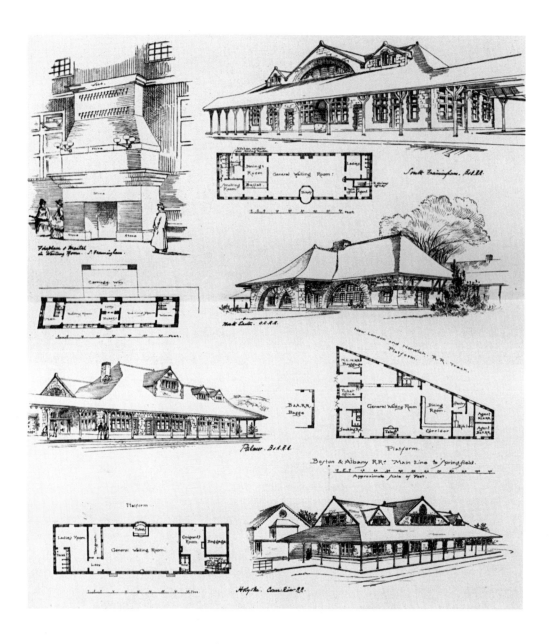

PLATE 62
"Sketch: Country House,"
Charles Edwards, *Amer-
ican Architect and Building
News*, Vol. 21, No. 584,
March 5, 1887. (Avery
Library, Columbia Univer-
sity)

PLATE 63
"Sketch for a small church
at Milford, MA," C.
Howard Walker, *Architec-
ture and Building*, Vol. 6,
No. 14, April 2, 1887.
(AIC)

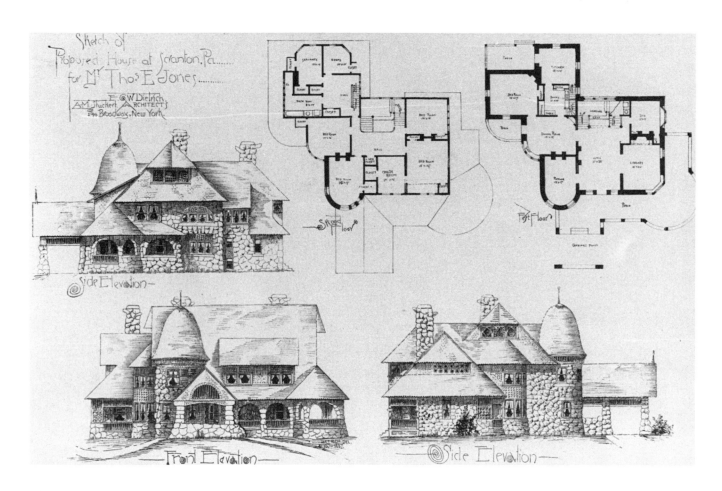

PLATE 64
"Sketch of Proposed House
at Scranton, PA, for Mr.
Thomas E. Jones, E.G.W.
Dietrich and A.M.
Stuckert, *Architecture and
Building*, Vol. 6, No. 15,
April 9, 1887. (AIC)

PLATE 65
"Summer Residence for Mr.
W.M. Terry [Sayville, LI],"
I.H. Green, *Architecture
and Building*, Vol. 6, No.
17, April 23, 1887. (AIC)

PLATE 66
"Hotel Lake Chatauqua,"
Clarence Luce, *Architecture
and Building*, Vol. 6, No.
20, May 14, 1887. (AIC)

PLATE 67
"Houses for Mrs. Cole
[Cleveland, OH]," C.O.
Arey Architects, *American
Architect and Building
News*, Vol. 21, No. 596,
May 28, 1887. (AIA
Archives)

HOTEL CUSHING'S ISLAND
Maine.

C. Luce Archt.
N.Y. City.

PLATE 68
"Hotel, Cushings Island,
ME," Clarence Luce, *Ar-
chitecture and Building*,
Vol. 7, No. 4, July 23,
1887. (AIC)

Lodge

PLATE 69
"Sketches of a House and
Lodge [Sea Coast of Ore-
gon]," Bertram Grosvenor
Goodhue, *Architecture and
Building*, Vol. 7, No. 4,
July 23, 1887. (AIC)

PLATE 70
"House for W. Moylan
Lansdale [Manchester,
PA]," Bertram Grosvenor
Goodhue, *American Archi-
tect and Building News*,
Vol. 21, No. 606, Aug. 6,
1887. (AIA Archives)

PLATE 71
"Half a Dozen Pen and Ink
Sketches," Bertram
Grosvenor Goodhue,
Architecture and Building,
Vol. 7, No. 10, Sept. 3,
1887. (AIC)

PLATE 72
"Sketches from Belle Isle
Park," Donaldson and
Meier, *American Architect
and Building News*, Aug.
13, 1887, Vol. 21, No. 607.
(AIA Archives)

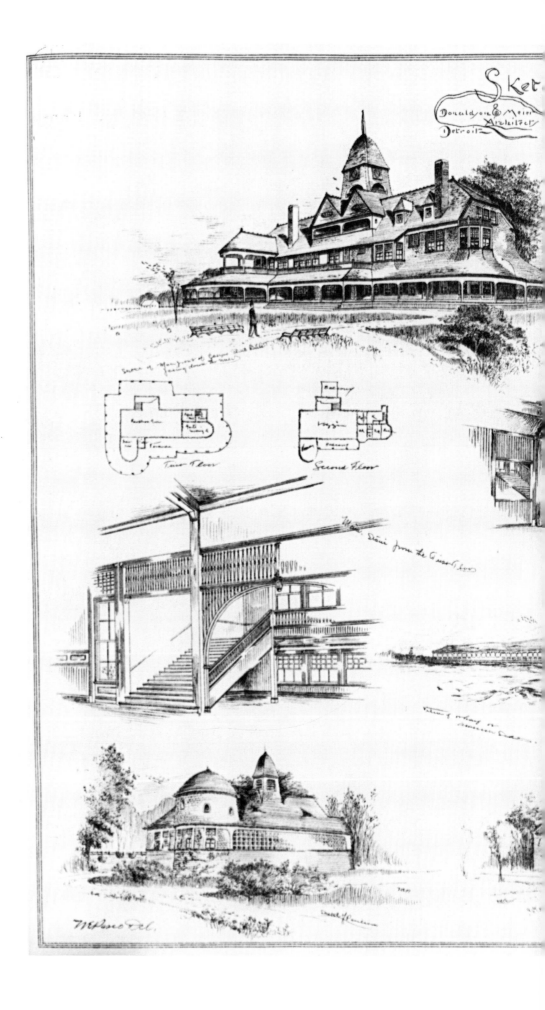

"Belle Isle Park"
near Detroit
Mich.

PLATE 73
"Residence at Rye on the
Sound," Bruce Price, *Ar-
chitecture and Building*,
Vol. 7, No. 16, Oct. 15,
1887. (AIC)

PLATE 74
"Union Chapel and Li-
brary, York Harbor, ME,"
William H. Dabney, *Architecture and Building*, Vol.
7, No. 19, Nov. 5, 1887.
(AIC)

FOR R. LASHHURST ESQ.
FARWOOD
OVERBROOK
PA.

WILSON EYRE ARCHT.
PHILADA, PENN.

Drawn from Photo by B R Tolman

PLATE 75
"House for R. Lashhurst [Farwood, Overbrook, PA]," Wilson Eyre, *Architecture and Building*, Vol. 7, No. 27, Dec. 31, 1887. (AIC)

PLATE 76
"House at Delano Park," John Calvin Stevens, *Architecture and Building*, Vol. 8, No. 6, Feb. 11, 1888. (AIC)

House at Delano Park
John Calvin Stevens Archt.

·BREEZYSIDE·BY·THE·SEA·
·GEO·MARTIN·HUSS·ARCH'T·

PLATE 77
"Breezyside by the Sea,"
George Martin Huss,
Architecture and Building,
Vol. 8, No. 7, Feb. 18,
1888. (AIC)

1887. Nov.
J.L.S.

House at Delano Park,
Cape Elizabeth, Me:

JOHN CALVIN STEVENS, ARCH'T.

PORTLAND, ME.

PLATE 78
"House at Delano Park
[Cape Elizabeth, ME],"
John Calvin Stevens, *Architecture and Building*, Vol.
8, No. 11, March 17, 1888.
(AIC)

DRAWING ROOM·   ·DINING ROOM·

·PLANTS·

·BUTLERS PANTRY·

·HALL·

·PANTRY·

·LIBRARY·   ·KITCHEN·

·SHED·

·PIAZZA·   ·V·   ·GROUND FLOOR PLAN·

·PORTE COCHERE·

SEAT

SEAT

PLATE 79
"House at Canton, Ohio,
for William S. Hawk,"
William A. Bates, *Architecture and Building*, Vol. 8,
No. 12, March 31, 1888.
(AIC)

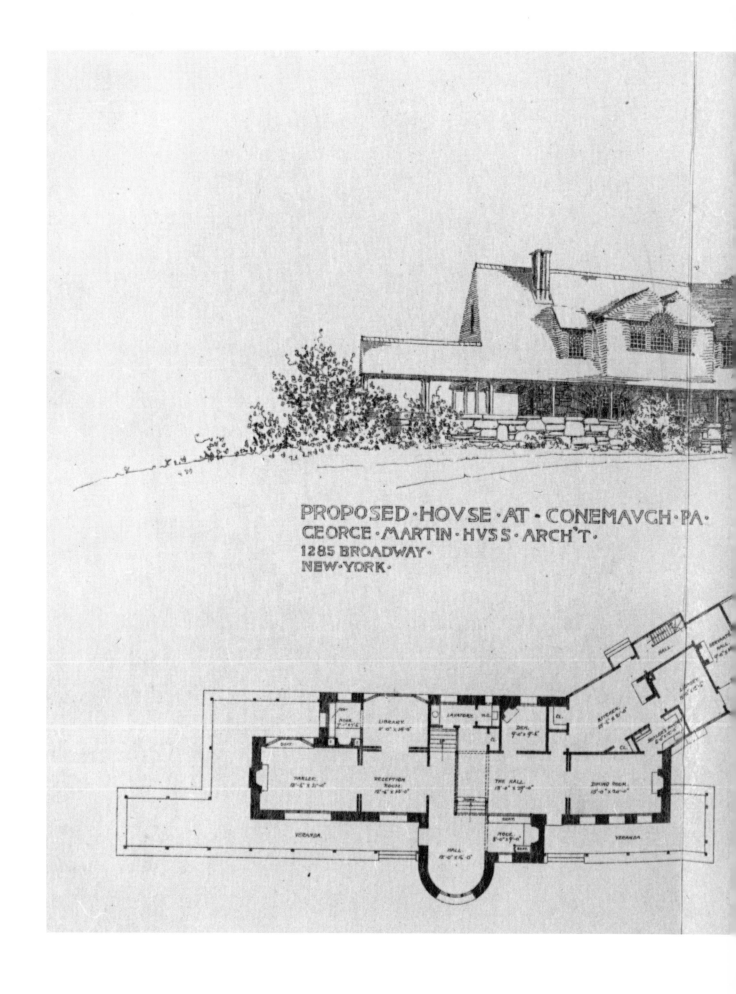

PROPOSED · HOVSE · AT · CONEMAVGH · PA ·
GEORGE · MARTIN · HVSS · ARCH'T ·
1285 BROADWAY ·
NEW · YORK ·

PLATE 80
"Proposed house at
Conemaugh, PA," George
Martin Huss, *Architecture
and Building*, Vol. 8, No.
17, April 28, 1888. (Avery
Library, Columbia University)

Cottage in Tuxedo Park
Bruce Price Arch't 74 W 23 St. N.Y.C

PLATE 81
"Cottage in Tuxedo Park,"
Bruce Price, *Architecture
and Building*, Vol. 8, No.
21, May 26, 1888. (AIC)

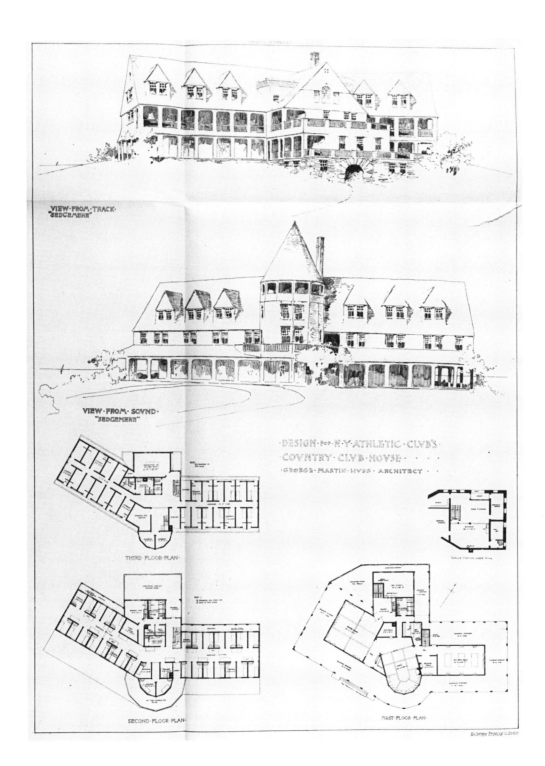

VIEW·FROM·TRACK· "SEDGEMERE"

VIEW·FROM·SOVND· "SEDGEMERE"

·DESIGN·for·N·Y·ATHLETIC·CLVB'S·
·COVNTRY·CLVB·HOVSE·
·GEORGE·MARTIN·HVSS·ARCHITECT·

THIRD·FLOOR·PLAN·

SECOND·FLOOR·PLAN·

FIRST·FLOOR·PLAN·

PLATE 82
"Design for the New York Athletic Club's Country Club House," George Martin Huss, *American Architect and Building News*, Vol. 23, No. 649, June 2, 1888. (AIA Archives)

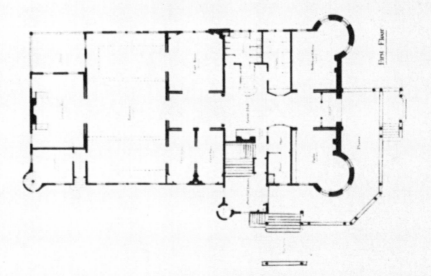

First Floor

Montclair

NE 30 1888

House
Lamb and Rich Architects

PLATE 83
"Montclair Clubhouse,"
Lamb and Rich, *Architecture and Building*, Vol. 8,
No. 26, June 30, 1888.
(AIC)

PLATE 84
"Design for a Country
Church," E.R. Tilton, *Ar-
chitecture and Building*,
Vol. 9, No. 1, July 7, 1888.
(AIC)

DESIGN FOR A COUNTRY CHURCH
E.R. TILTON ARCH'T   23 WARREN ST NEW-YORK

PLATE 85
"A Hotel at Little Falls,
MN," Gilbert and Taylor,
*American Architect and
Building News*, Vol. 14,
No. 655, July 14, 1888.
(AIA Archives)

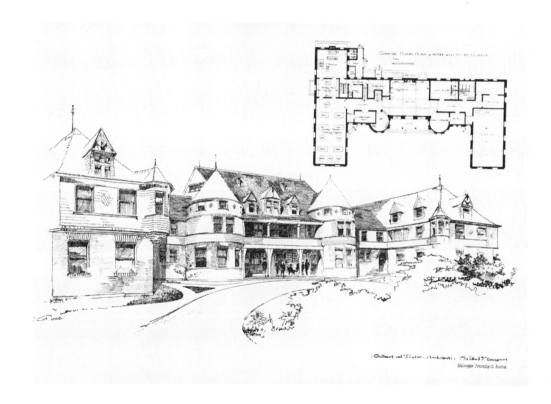

PLATE 86
"House for George
Griswold at Tuxedo,"
William A. Bates, *Architecture and Building*, Vol. 9,
No. 2, July 14, 1888.
(AIC)

PLATE 87
"Gate Lodge at Fanwood,
NJ," McKim, Mead and
White, *Architecture and
Building*, Vol. 9, No. 2,
July 14, 1888. (AIC)

PLATE 88
"Summer Headquarters of the Portland Club [Great Diamond Island, ME]," John Calvin Stevens, *Architecture and Building*, Vol. 9, No. 6, Aug. 11, 1888. (AIC)

PLATE 89
"Residence of A. G. Kennedy [Minneapolis, MN]," L.S. Buffington, *American Architect and Building News*, Vol. 24, No. 671, Nov. 3, 1888. (AIA Archives)

PLATE 90
"Residence for A. L.
Wilsten [Lynchburg, VA],"
L.S. Buffington, *Inland
Architect*, Vol. 12, No. 7,
Dec. 1888. (AIC)

PLATE 91
"Pen and Ink Sketches at Swampscott, MA; Grass Head House," Arthur Little, *Architecture and Building*, Vol. 9, No. 25, Dec. 22, 1888. (AIC)

92

Residence of Col. Wᵐ L Brown
Great Barrington. Mass

PLATE 92
"Residence of Colonel
William L. Brown," A.
Page Brown, *Architecture
and Building*, Vol. 10, No.
5, Feb. 2, 1889. (AIC)

PLATE 93
"Country Club House,"
Little and O'Conner, *Architecture and Building*,
Vol. 10, No. 11, March 16,
1889. (AIC)

ROBERTA WELKE PHOTO-LITH 176 WILLIAM ST N.Y

Eleva

ng Water.

PLATE 95
"Gate Lodge for G. A.
Nickerson [Dedham,
MA]," Longfellow, Alden
and Harlow, *American Architect and Building News*,
Vol. 25, No. 695, April 20,
1889. (AIA Archives)

PLATE 96
"House of B. E. Taylor
[Newton, MA]," Rand and
Taylor, *American Architect
and Building News*, Vol.
25, No. 696, April 27,
1889. (AIA Archives)

PLATE 97
"Gate Lodge for the Montana Agricultural, Mineral and Mechanical Association [Helena, Montana]," Heins and La Farge, *Architecture and Building*, Vol. 10, No. 23, June 8, 1889. (AIC)

PLATE 98
"House at Lansdowne for
A. J. Drexel, Jr.," Wilson
Eyre, *American Architect
and Building News*, Vol.
25, No. 698, May 11, 1889.
(AIA Archives)

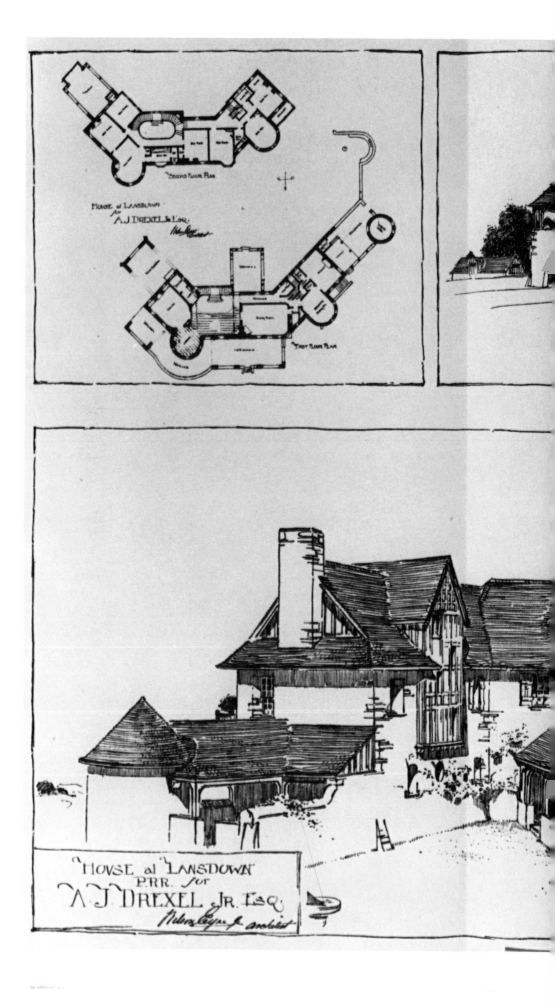

VIEW FROM THE SOUTH.

W. Eyre del.

VIEW FROM THE NORTH.

W. Eyre del.

PLATE 99
"House in Germantown,"
Wilson Eyre, *Architecture
and Building*, Vol. 10, No.
24, June 15, 1889. (AIC)

HOUSE IN GERMANTOWN.
WILSON EYRE JR. ARCH.

SOVTH WEST. VIE   wEyre del.

NORTH EAST VIEW.

PLATE 100
"House and Stable at
Haverford College Sta-
tion," Wilson Eyre, *Amer-
ican Architect and Building
News*, Vol. 25, No. 705,
June 29, 1889. (AIA Ar-
chives)

PLATE 101
"Ice House for Country
Place of Col. William L.
Brown, "[Great Bar-
rington, MA]," A. Page
Brown, Willis Polk, del.,
Architecture and Building,
Vol. 11, No. 1, July 6,
1889. (AIC)

PLATE 102
"Stable for Country
Place of Col. William L.
Brown," A. Page Brown,
Willis Polk, del., *Architec-
ture and Building*, Vol. 11,
No. 1, July 6, 1889. (AIC)

Within the illustration:
· SECOND · PRIZE ·

BUILDING SKETCH CLUB'S COMPETITION ~ SUBMITTED BY "FAR FROM THE MADDING CROWD" · CLAUDE · F · BRAGDON ·

ROBERT A. WELKE, PHOTO-LITH 178 WILLIAM ST. N.Y.

PLATE 103
"Building Sketch Club's Competition, 2nd Prize, submitted by 'Far from the Madding Crowd,'" Claude F. Bragdon, *Architecture and Building*, Vol. 11, No. 4, July 27, 1889. (Avery Library, Columbia University)

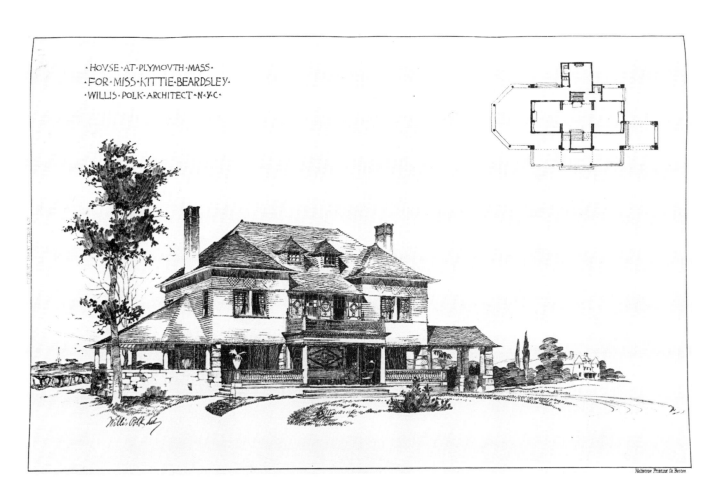

·HOVSE·AT·PLYMOVTH·MASS·
·FOR·MISS·KITTIE·BEARDSLEY·
·WILLIS·POLK·ARCHITECT·N·Y·C·

PLATE 104
"House at Plymouth,
Mass. for Miss Kittie
Beardsley," Willis Polk,
*American Architect and
Building News*, Vol. 26,
No. 709, July 27, 1889.
(AIA Archives)

PLATE 105
"Old People's Home,"
A. Page Brown, *Architecture and Building*, Vol. 11,
No. 4, July 27, 1889.
(Avery Library, Columbia
University)

PLATE 106
"Sketch showing Theatre
Addition to Bar Harbor
Casino, [ME]" Wilson
Eyre, *Architecture and
Building*, Vol. 11, No. 8,
Aug. 24, 1889. (AIC)

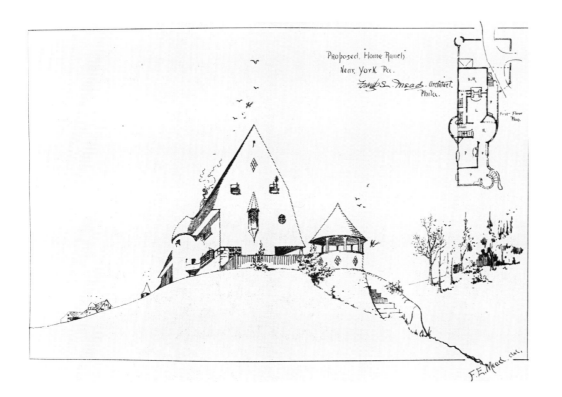

Proposed 'Home Ranch'
Near, York, Pa.

Frank S. Mead. Architect.
Phila.

PLATE 107
"Proposed 'Home Ranch' near York, PA," Frank S. Mead, *American Architect and Building News*, Vol. 26, No. 714, Aug. 31, 1889. (AIA Archives)

Sketches for Cottages in Colorado Springs

Mellen, Westell and Kirby
Architects
55 Broadway
N.Y.

PLATE 108
"Sketches for Cottages in Colorado Springs," Mellen, Westell and Kirby, *Architecture and Building*, Vol. 11, No. 21, Sept. 21, 1889. (AIC)

PLATE 109
"House for Francis W.
Kennedy, Esq. at Bradford
Hills, PA," Frank Miles
Day, *American Architect
and Building News*, Vol.
26, No. 725, Nov. 16,
1889. (AIA Archives)

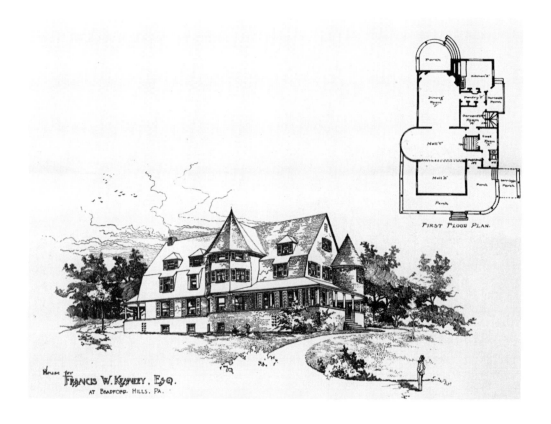

FIRST FLOOR PLAN.

House for FRANCIS W. KENNEDY, ESQ.
AT BRADFORD HILLS, PA.

Residence on Harper Tract.
Los Angeles, California

PLATE 110
"Residence on Harper Tract
Los Angeles, CA," W. Red-
mire Ray, *American Architect and Building News*,
Vol. 26, No. 731, Dec. 28,
1889. (AIA Archives)

PLATE 111
"Residence for Grosse
Pointe, MI," Mason and
Rice, *Inland Architect*, Vol.
14, No. 7, Dec. 1889.
(AIC)

PLATE 112
"Edwin D. Morgan house,
'Wheatley Hills,'"
1890–91, 1898–1900,
(McKim, Mead, and White
Archives, New-York His-
torical Society)

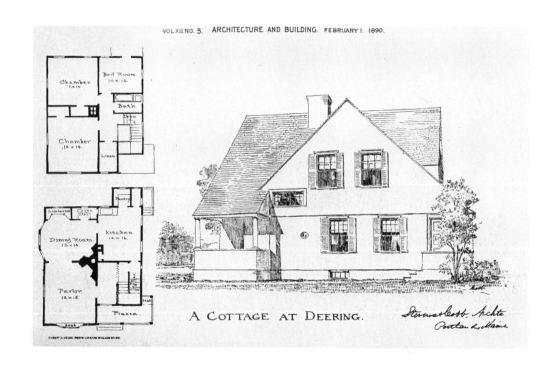

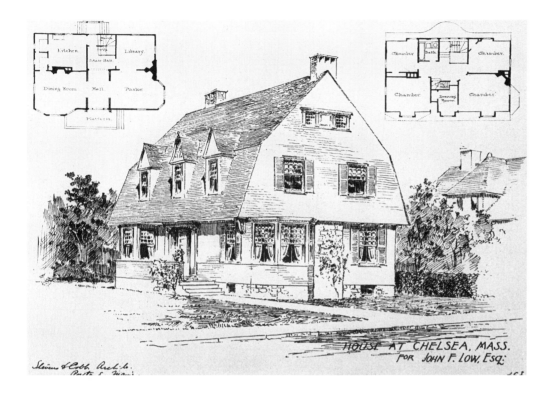

PLATE 115
"House at Chelsea, MA,"
Stevens and Cobb, *Architecture and Building*, Vol. 12, No. 5, Feb. 1, 1890. (AIC)

PLATE 116
"House of H. Casimir de Rham [Tuxedo Park, NY],"
William A. Bates, *Architecture and Building*, Vol. 12, No. 10, March 8, 1890. (AIC)

PLATE 117
"Residence of A.H. Stem
[Minnetonka Beach,
MN]," *American Architect
and Building News*, Vol.
27, No. 741, March 8,
1890. (AIA Archives)

PLATE 118
"A Cottage at Tuxedo,"
Renwick, Aspinwall, and
Russell, *American Architect
and Building News*, Vol.
27, No. 744, March 29,
1890. (AIA Archives)

A·COTTAGE·AT·
TVXEDO··
RENWICK·ASPINWALL·&·RVSSELL
ARCH'TS·71·BRDWAY·N.Y.

PLATE 119
"House for F.W. Rosenthal
[Alameda, CA]," Willis
Polk, *Architecture and
Building*, Vol. 12, No. 15,
April 12, 1890. (AIC)

PLATE 120
"Summer House for Mr.
H. McMillan, Grosse
Pointe [MI]," Mason and
Rice, *American Architect
and Building News*, Vol.
28, No. 755, June 14, 1890.
(AIA Archives)

Sketch of Windmill etc.
for L.A. Emery. Ellsworth, Me.

John Calvin Stevens
Albert Winslow Cobb) Arch'ts.

J.C.S.

From the Boston Architectural Club Exhibition

Heliotype Printing Co. Boston.

PLATE 121
"Sketch of Windmill, etc.,
for L.A. Emery, Ellsworth,
Me.," John Calvin Stevens,
Albert Winslow Cobb,
*American Architect and
Building News*, Vol. 28,
No. 755, June 14, 1890.
(AIA Archives)

PLATE 122
"Lake St. Clair Fishing and
Shooting Club on Lake St.
Clair, Michigan," Rogers
and MacFarlane, *American
Architect and Building
News*, Vol. 29, No. 758,
July 5, 1890. (AIA
Archives)

Original Sketch for "Pontefract Inn" Conn. — Hoppin, Read & Hoppin Arch'ts — Providence R.I.

PLATE 124
"Proposed Houses on Park
Ave. for John O. Heald,
Esq. [Orange, NJ]],"
Edward Hapgood, *Archi-
tecture and Building*, Vol.
14, No. 5, Jan. 31, 1891.
(AIC)

PLATE 125
"House at Buffalo for Mrs.
Anna Hoxie Cook," C.D.
Swan, *American Architect
and Building News*, Vol.
31, No. 789, Feb. 7, 1891.
(AIA Archives)

PLATE 126
"Church of St. John the Evangelist [San Francisco, CA]," 1890–91, Longstreth, Richard, *On the Edge of the World.* (Photograph by John Beach, courtesy of Richard Longstreth)

PLATE 127
"Proposed Hotel at Lake George, N.Y.," Frank T. Cornell, *Architecture and Building*, Vol. 14, No. 10, March 7, 1891. (AIC)

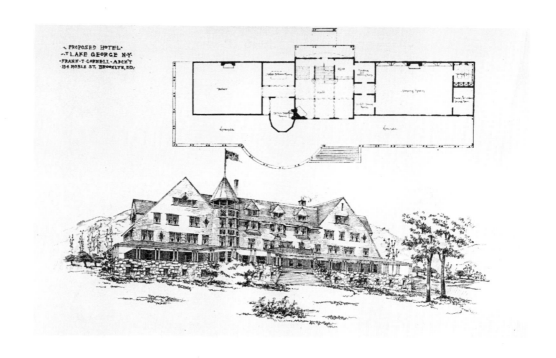

PLATE 128
"House at 'Acorn Point,' Manitou Island, near St. Paul, Minnesota," Gilbert and Taylor, Cass Gilbert, del.; *American Architect and Building News*, Vol. 32, No. 804, May 23, 1891. (AIA Archives)

PLATE 129
"A Mountain Church,"
E. Eldon Deane, *American Architect and Building News*, Vol. 32, No. 804, May 23, 1891. (AIA Archives)

PLATE 130
"The New Inn at
Ridgefield, Conn.,"
William A. Bates, *American Architect and Building
News*, Vol. 33, No. 810,
July 4, 1891. (AIA
Archives)

THE·NEW·INN·AT·RIDGEFIELD, CONN·
WILLIAM·A·BATES, ARCHITECT·····
149·BROADWAY, NEW YORK CITY····

Ground Floor Plan.

PLATE 131
"The Newton Club (An
unaccepted design)," Jarvis
Hunt, *American Architect
and Building News*, Vol.
33, No. 816, Aug. 15,
1891. (AIA Archives)

PLATE 132
"A Picturesque Suburban
Railroad Station on the
C. M. and St. P. R.R.,
Sheridan Park, Chicago,
IL," Holabird and Roche,
Sketches by E. Eldon
Deane, *Inland Architect*,
Vol. 19, No. 2, March
1892. (AIA Archives)

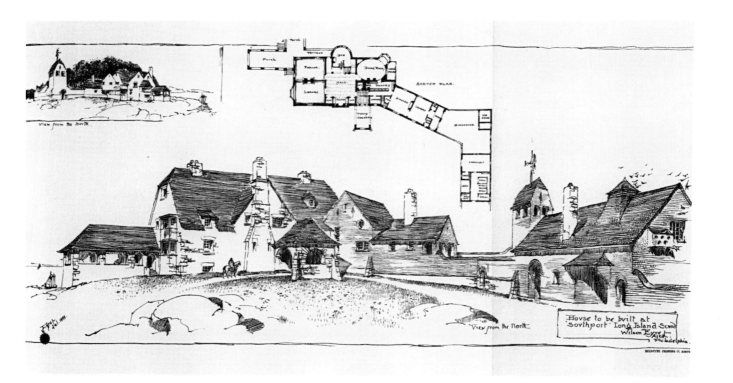

PLATE 133
"A House to be built at 'Southport,' Long Island Sound," Wilson Eyre. *American Architect and Building News*, Vol. 36, No. 858, June 4, 1892. (AIA Archives)

PLATE 134
"House for Messrs. Wendell and Smith," Horace Trumbauer, *American Architect and Building News*, Vol. 36, No. 861, June 25, 1892. (AIA Archives)

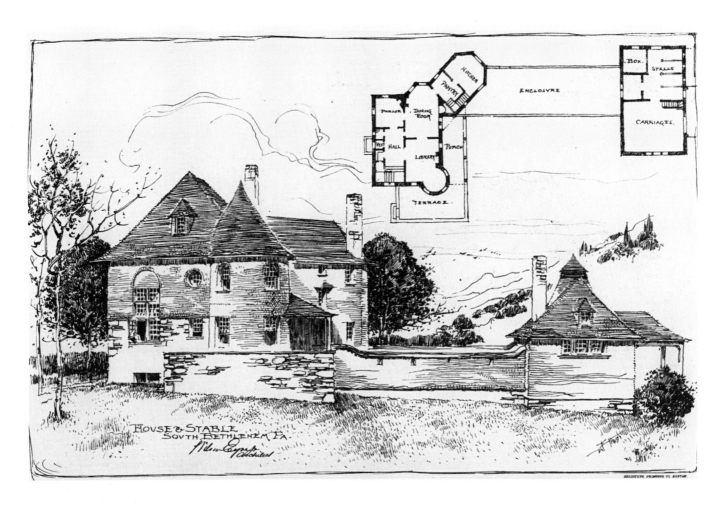

Within the drawing:

ENCLOSURE

BOX

STALLS

CARRIAGES.

KITCHEN

PANTRY

PARLOR

DINING ROOM

WEST HALL

LIBRARY

PORCH

TERRACE

HOUSE & STABLE
SOUTH BETHLEHEM PA

Wilson Eyre
Architect

PLATE 135
"House and Stable, South
Bethlehem, PA," Wilson
Eyre, *American Architect
and Building News*, Vol.
37, No. 863, July 9, 1892.
(AIA Archives)

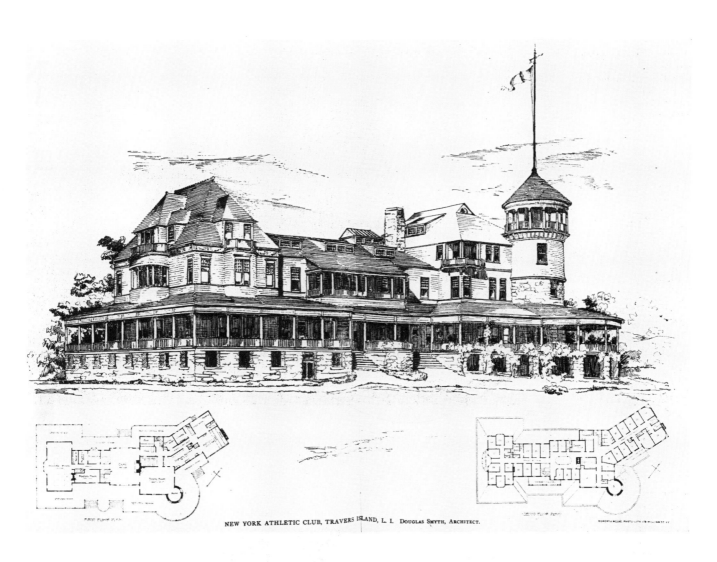

NEW YORK ATHLETIC CLUB, TRAVERS ISLAND, L. I. DOUGLAS SMYTH, ARCHITECT.

PLATE 136
"New York Athletic Club,
Travers Island, L.I.,"
Douglas Smyth, *Architecture and Building*, Vol. 17,
No. 3, July 16, 1892.
(Marquand Library, Princeton University)

PLATE 137
"Cottage for M.E. Ingalls,
Hot Springs, Virginia,"
G.W.E. Field, *Inland Architect*, Vol. 21, No. 2,
March 1893. (AIA
Archives)

PLATE 138
"Front View of Cottage for
M.E. Ingalls, Hot Springs,
Virginia," G.W.E. Field,
Inland Architect, Vol. 21,
No. 4, May 1893. (AIA
Archives)

PLATE 139
"Laundry Building, Hot
Springs, Virginia," G.W.E.
Field, *Inland Architect*,
Vol. 21, No. 2, March
1893. (AIA Archives)

PLATE 140
"Bowling Alley, Hot
Springs, Virginia," G.W.E.
Field, *Inland Architect*,
Vol. 21, No. 4, May 1893.
(AIA Archives)

PLATE 141
"Residence of D. E. Taylor,
Scranton, Pennsylvania,"
E.G.W. Dietrich, *Inland
Architect*, Vol. 21, No. 3,
April 1893. (AIA Archives)

"Lancashire Inn"

E.G.W. Dietrich Architect
18 Broadway New York

PLATE 142
"Lancashire Inn," E.G.W.
Dietrich, *American Archi-
tect and Building News*,
Vol. 40, No. 902, April 8,
1893. (AIA Archives)

COTTAGE AT EDEN FLORIDA
FOR
MR. WILLIAM DE LUNA.
CHAS. H. ISRAELS ARCH'T. 30 NASSAU ST. N.Y.

PLAN.

PLATE 143
"Cottage at Eden, Florida,
for Mr. William De Luna,"
Charles H. Israels, *Architecture and Building*, Vol.
38, No. 17, April 29, 1893.
(Marquand Library, Princeton University)

PLATE 144
" 'Glengarriff,' Seal Harbor, Me., for Mr. Geo. B. Cooksey," I.H. Green, Jr., *Architecture and Building*, Vol. 19, No. 6, Aug. 5, 1893. (Marquand Library, Princeton University)

"GLENGARRIFF," SEAL HARBOR, ME

FOR MR. GEO. B. COOKSEY.   I.H. GREEN, JR.,
ARCHITECT, SAYVILLE, N.Y.

FIRST FLOOR.

Servant's Hall

Servant's Porch

Kitchen

Hall Room

Dining Room

Entrance Hall

Bed Room

Living Room

Veranda

Entry

Loggia.

Alcove.

Staircase Alcove

Carriage Porch

C.K.Birdsall, Del. 1893.

PLATE 145
"Cottage at Tuxedo for
Ballard Smith Esq.," James
Brown Lord, *American Ar-
chitect and Building News*,
Vol. 42, No. 930, Oct. 21,
1893. (AIA Archives)

HOUSE FOR MR YOUNG NEAR ST LOUIS
EAMES AND YOUNG ARCHITECTS

PLATE 146
"House for Mr. Young near St. Louis," Eames and Young, *American Architect and Building News*, Vol. 42, No. 934, Nov. 18, 1893. (AIA Archives)

·•·THE SCHOOL HOUSE·‹‹‹
•BAY RIDGE, L.I.•
·PARFITT BROS·} ASSOCIATED •
·WM·A·BATES·} ARCHITECTS•
AND

J·A·JOHNSON 93

HELIOTYPE PRINTING C°. BOSTON

PLATE 148
"Country Club-House on
Long Island, NY," Douglas
Smyth and A.R. McIlvaine,
*American Architect and
Building News*, Vol. 43,
No. 951, March 17, 1894.
(AIA Archives)

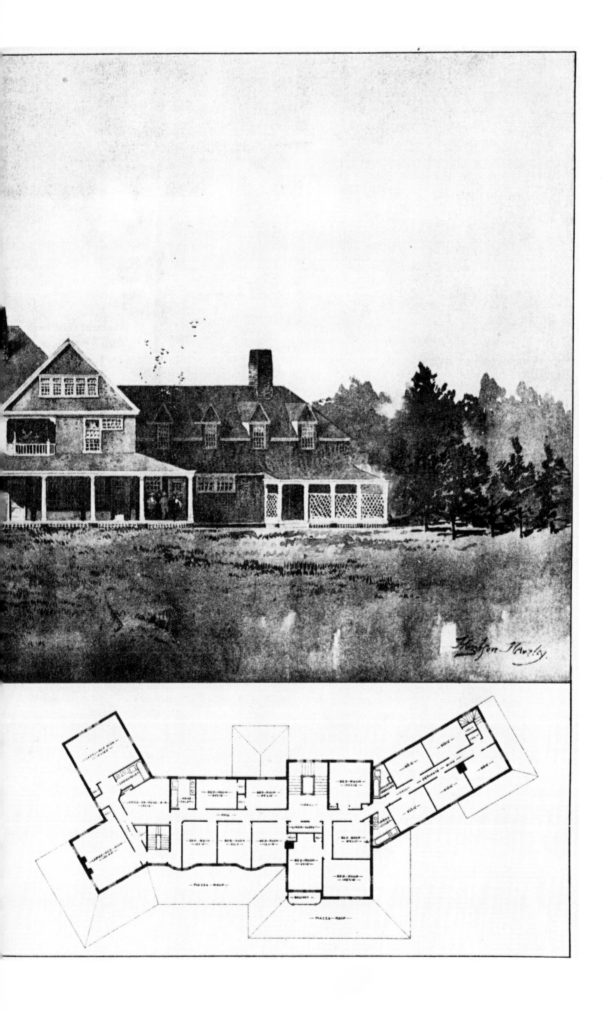

PLATE 149
"Casino at West Hartford,"
F.R. Comstock, *American
Architect and Building
News*, Vol. 44, No. 957,
April 28, 1894. (AIA
Archives)

PLATE 150
"Proposed Country House
for David Pepper [Chestnut
Hill, PA]," Wilson Eyre,
*American Architect and
Building News*, Vol. 44,
No. 962, June 2, 1894.
(AIA Archives)

·BVRLINGAME·COVNTRY·CLVB·STABLE·

PLATE 151
"Burlingame Country Club
Stable," A. Page Brown,
*American Architect and
Building News*, Vol. 46,
No. 985, Nov. 10, 1894.
(AIA Archives)

PLATE 152
"City of Boston, Shelter
and Look-Out at Castle Island," Edmund Wheel-
wright, E.D. MagInnes,
del., *American Architect
and Building News*, Vol.
46, No. 990, Dec. 15,
1894. (AIA Archives)

PLATE 153
"Residence of Judge
Elliot," Pond and Pond,
Inland Architect, Vol. 25,
No. 4, May 1895. (AIA
Archives)

PLATE 154
"Plan of Demelman Park,
Winthrop Beach, Frontage
Directly Upon the Ocean,"
A.W. Cobb, *Architecture
and Building*, Vol. 22, No.
3, June 8, 1895. (AIC)

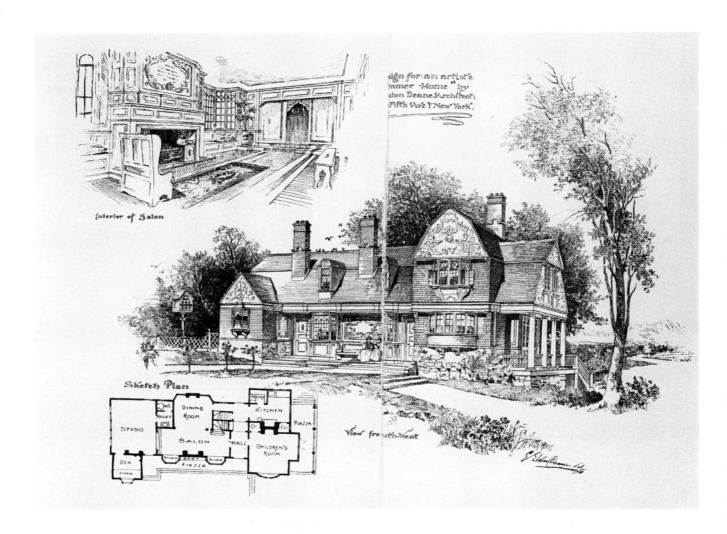

Interior of Salon

ign for an artist's
mmer Home," by
don Deane, Architect:
Fifth Ave & New York.

Sketch Plan

STUDIO
TOILET
DINING ROOM
PANTRY
KITCHEN
PIAZZA
SALON
HALL
CHILDREN'S ROOM
DEN
DIVAN SEAT DIVAN
PIAZZA
DIVAN
Cc
Cc

View from South West

PLATE 155
"Design for an Artist's
Summer Home," E. Eldon
Deane, *Inland Architect*,
Vol. 26, No. 5, Dec. 1895.
(AIA Archives)

PLATE 156
"Studies for Country
Houses," Frank E. Wallis,
Architecture and Building,
Vol. 24, No. 1, January 4,
1896. (AIC)

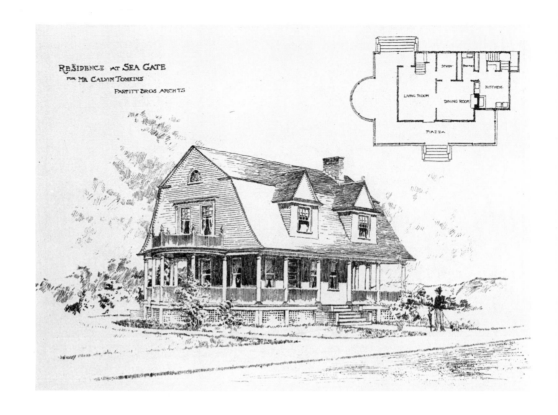

PLATE 159
"Gate House and Office at Sea Gate, LI, for Norton Point Land Co.," Parfitt Brothers, E. Werner, del.; *Architecture and Building*, Vol. 25, No. 25, Dec. 19, 1896. (AIA Archives)

PLATE 160
"Dexter Brothers' English Shingle Stain," [Advertisement] *Inland Architect*, Vol. 29, No. 2, March 1897. (AIC)

PLATE 163
Residence of Hon. Wm. A. Fisher, Ruxton, Md.," Wyatt and Nolting, *Architecture and Building*, Vol. 26, No. 25, June 19, 1897. (AIC)

PLATE 164
"Residence of William Painter, Esq., Pikeville, MD," Wyatt and Nolting, *Architecture and Building*, Vol. 26, No. 25, June 19, 1897. (AIA Archives)

PLATE 165
"House at Quogue, L.I.,"
W. Gedney Beatty, *Architecture and Building*, Vol.
27, No. 25, Dec. 18, 1897.
(Marquand Library, Princeton University)

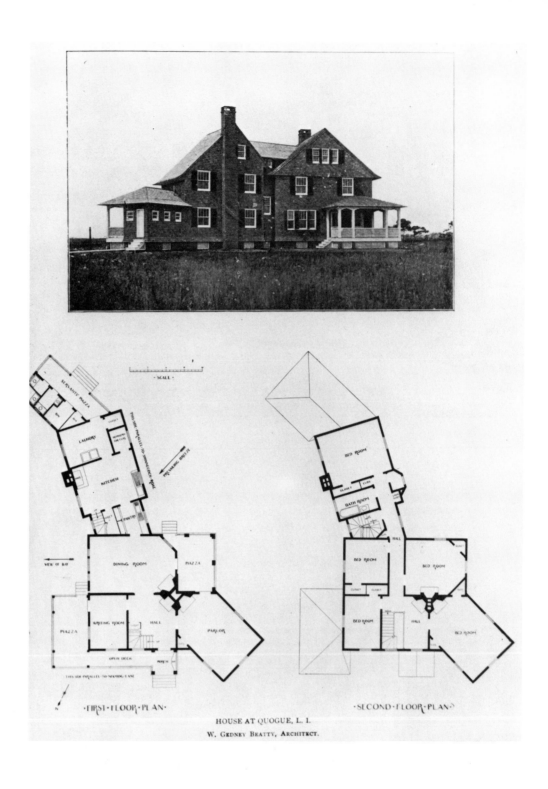

HOUSE AT QUOGUE, L. I.
W. Gedney Beatty, Architect.

PLATE 166
"Administration and Department Buildings, Connecticut Childrens Aid Society," F.R. Comstock, *Architecture and Building*, Vol. 27, No. 13, Sept. 25, 1897. (Marquand Library, Princeton University)

HOUSES FOR OPERATIVES AT HOPEDALE, MASS.

PLATE 167
"Houses for Operatives at Hopedale, Mass.," developed by the Drapers, *Architecture and Building*, Vol. 27, No. 19, Nov. 6, 1897. (Marquand Library, Princeton University)

PLATE 168
"Residence of Mrs. Frank
Bradley [Evanston, IL],"
W. Chester Chase, *Inland
Architect*, Vol. 31, No. 3,
April 1898. (AIC)

PLATE 169
"Residence of Mrs. Frank
Bradley [Evanston, IL],"
W. Chester Chase, *Inland
Architect*, Vol. 31, No. 4,
May 1898. (AIC)

PLATE 170
"Residence of Mr. Burnett,
[Evanston, IL]," F.P. Burn-
ham Co., *Inland Architect*,
Vol. 31, No. 3, April 1898.
(AIC)

PLATE 171
"Residence for A.H. Gross
[Evanston, IL]," Flanders
and Zimmerman, *Inland
Architect*, Vol. 31, No. 3,
April 1898. (AIC)

PLATE 172
"Rockaway Hunt Club
[Cedarhurst, LI]," Lord,
Hewlett and Hull, *Inland
Architect*, Vol. 32, No. 3,
Oct. 1898. (AIC)

PLATE 173
"Lounging Room, Rock-
away Hunt Club," Lord,
Hewlett, and Hull, *Inland
Architect*, Vol. 32, No. 3,
Oct. 1898. (AIC)

PLATE 174
"House for Mr. C.D.
Thompson, Montclair,
N.J.," Frank E. Wallis, *Ar-
chitecture and Building*,
Vol. 29, No. 7, Aug. 13,
1898. (AIA Archives)

Plate 175
"Gate Lodge, Entrance and
Stables to 'Laddins Rock'
Farm, Sound Beach,
Conn.," Alfred H. Taylor,
Architecture and Building,
Vol. 29, No. 16, Oct. 15,
1898. (AIA Archives)

PLATE 176
"House of B. Frank Wood,
[Pasadena, CA]," H. Ridge-
way, *American Architect
and Building News*, Vol.
64, No. 1216, April 15,
1899. (AIA Archives)

PLATE 177
"House of Thomas S.
Wotkyns [Pasadena, CA],"
F.L. Roehrig, *American Ar-
chitect and Building News*,
Vol. 64, No. 1222, May 27,
1899. (AIA Archives)

PLATE 178
"House of Jason Evans [Pasadena, CA]," Blick and Moore, *American Architect and Building News*, Vol. 64, No. 1222, May 27, 1899. (AIA Archives)

· RESIDENCE · OF · GEORGE · GRISWOLD · ESQ ·
· TUXEDO · PARK ·
· WILLIAM · A · BATES · · ARCHITECT ·

PLATE 179
"Residence of George Griswold [Tuxedo Park, NY]," William A. Bates, *American Architect and Building News*, Vol. 65, No. 1228, July 8, 1899. (AIA Archives)

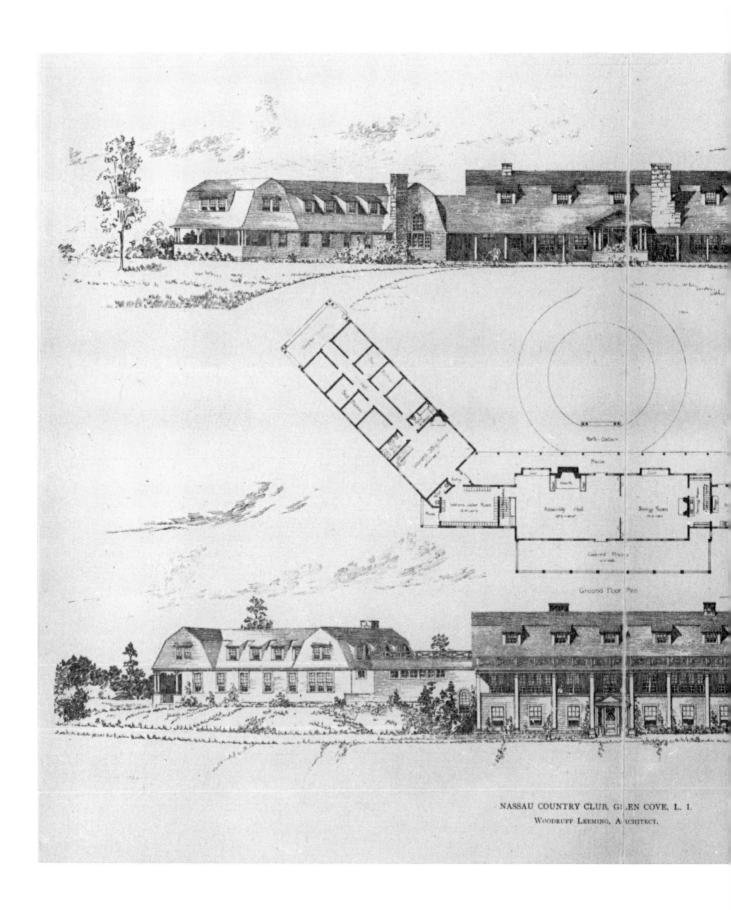

NASSAU COUNTRY CLUB, GLEN COVE, L. I.
WOODRUFF LEEMING, ARCHITECT.

PLATE 180
"Nassau Country Club
[Glen Cove, LI]," Wood-
ruff Leeming, *Architecture
and Building*, Vol. 31, No.
3, July 15, 1899. (Avery
Library, Columbia Univer-
sity)

PLATE 181
"Residence of Dr. N. S.
Davis [Lake Forest, IL],"
Howard Van Doren Shaw,
Inland Architect, Vol. 33,
No. 6, July 1899. (AIC)

PLATE 182
"House for Marshall C.
Lefferts [Cedarhurst, LI],"
Lord, Hewlett and Hull,
Vol. 34, No. 2, *Inland Ar-
chitect*, Sept. 1899. (AIC)

PLATE 183
"Residence of Geo. D.
Pratt, Glen Cove, L.I.,
Rear View," W.B. Tubby,
*Architect's and Builder's
Magazine*, Vol. 1 (32), No.
2; Nov. 1899. (AIA
Archives)

PLATE 184
"Stone Cliff Cottage, Bid-
deford Pool, [ME]," Albert
W. Cobb, *Architect's and
Builder's Magazine*, Vol. 1
(32), No. 4, Jan. 1900.
(AIA Archives)

PLATE 187
"House for Craig Heber-
ton, Camp Hill, Pa.,"
Wilson Eyre, *Inland Architect*, Vol. 35, No. 3, April
1900. (AIA Archives)

PLATE 188
"Cottage, Germantown,
PA," Wilson Eyre, *Inland
Architect*, Vol. 35, No. 3,
April 1900. (AIA Archives)

PLATE 189
"House of A.G. Hyde
[Larchmont, NY],"
Ludlow and Valentine,
*American Architect and
Building News*, Vol. 69,
No. 1280, July 7, 1900.
(AIA Archives)

PLATE 190
"House of Charles H.
Coster [Tuxedo Park, NY],
Entrance Front," W.A.
Bates, *American Architect
and Building News*, Vol.
69, No. 1291, Sept. 22,
1900. (AIA Archives)

PLATE 191
"House of Charles H.
Coster [Tuxedo Park, NY],
Rear View," W.A. Bates,
*American Architect and
Building News*, Vol. 69,
No. 1291, Sept. 22, 1900.
(AIA Archives)

PLATE 192
" 'Gray Arches,' [Lawrence
Park, Bronxville, NY],
Rear View," W.A. Bates,
*American Architect and
Building News*, Vol. 69,
No. 1291, Sept. 22, 1900.
(AIA Archives)

PLATE 193
"The Casino, Lawrence Park, Bronxville, NY," W.A. Bates, *American Architect and Building News*, Vol. 70, No. 1296, Oct. 27, 1900. (AIA Archives)

HOUSE OF J. F. MORSE ESQ., ROXBURY, MASS.

HOUSE OF J. F. MORSE ESQ., ROXBURY, MASS.

STABLE FOR S. W. JANES CLIFTON, MASS.

HOUSE OF C. S. DENNISON, NEWTONVILLE, MASS.

HOUSE OF C. P. FLAGG ESQ., BROOKLINE MASS.

PLATE 194
"Suburban Houses," J.A. Schweinfurth, *American Architect and Building News*, Vol. 70, No. 1305, Dec. 29, 1900. (AIA Archives)

PLATE 197
"Grenville Arms, [photograph, Bayhead, NJ],"
Wilson Eyre, *American Architect and Building News*, Vol. 74, No. 1351, Nov. 16, 1901. (AIA Archives)

PLATE 198
"Grenville Arms, [drawing, Bayhead, NJ]; Wilson Eyre, *American Architect and Building News*, Vol. 74, No. 1351, Nov. 16, 1901. (AIA Archives)

PLATE 199
E. Wiler Churchill House,
[Napa, CA], Coxhead and
Coxhead, 1892, Overland
Monthly, Vol. 29, No. 4,
April 1902. (Marquand Li-
brary, Princeton Univer-
sity)

PLATE 200
"Residence, Los Angeles,
Cal.," Inland Architect,
Vol. 39, No. 3, April 1902.
(AIA Archives)

PLATE 201
"Residence at Los Angeles, Cal.," Hunt and Eager, *Inland Architect*, Vol. 39, No. 5, June 1902. (AIA Archives)

PLATE 202
"Residence, Los Angeles, CA," Locke and Munsell, *Inland Architect*, Vol. 41, No. 1, Feb. 1903. (AIC)

PLATE 203
"An Artistic Cottage [Prospect Heights, Nutley, NJ]," William A. Lambert, *Architect's and Builder's Magazine*, Vol. 4 (35), No. 10, July 1903. (Avery Library, Columbia University)

PLATE 204
"Residence of Judge Scarrett [Kansas City, MO],"
Frank Hill, *Inland Architect*, Vol. 42, No. 1, Aug. 1903. (AIC)

PLATE 205
"The Modern American Dwelling—Exemplifying Fashion," Jay Wheeler Dow, *Architect's and Builder's Magazine*, Vol. 4 (35), No. 12, Sept. 1903. (Avery Library, Columbia University)

PLATE 206
"Sketch for Chapter
House, Psi Upsilon Frater-
nity, Bowdoin College,"
John Calvin Stevens, *Amer-
ican Architect and Building
News*, Vol. 82, No. 1449,
Oct. 3, 1903. (AIA Ar-
chives)

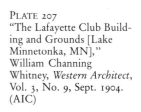

PLATE 207
"The Lafayette Club Building and Grounds [Lake Minnetonka, MN]," William Channing Whitney, *Western Architect*, Vol. 3, No. 9, Sept. 1904. (AIC)

PLATE 208
"Residence of Mr. John K. Williams [Hartford, CT]," E.G.W. Dietrich, *Architect's and Builder's Magazine*, Vol. 6 (37), No. 3, Dec. 1904. (AIC)

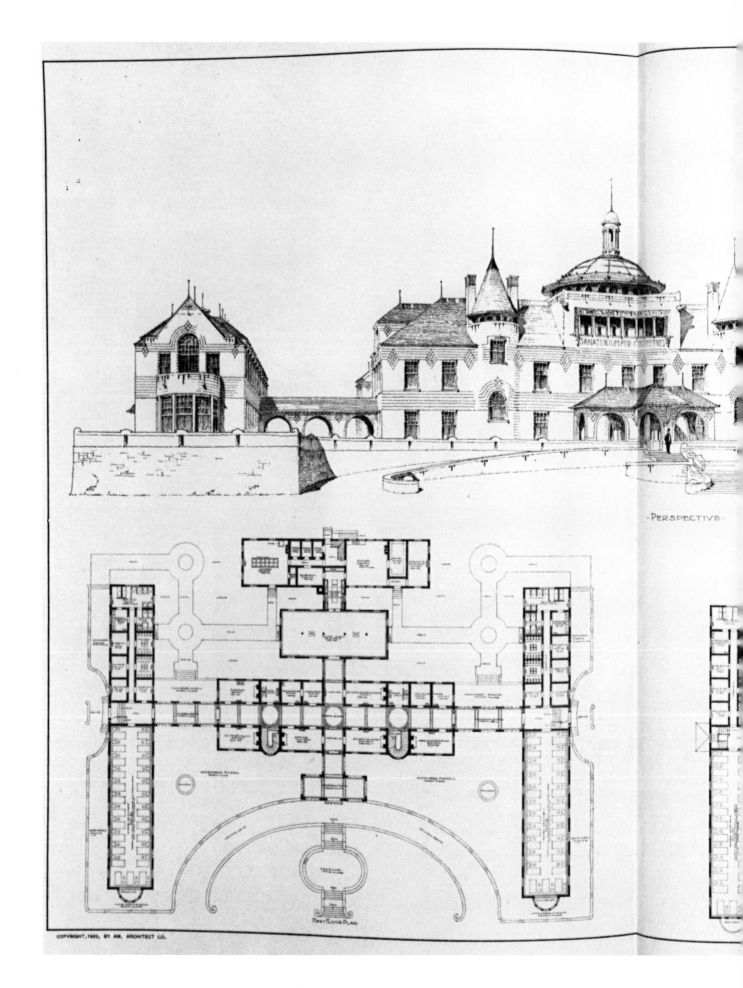

PERSPECTIVE

SANATORIUM FOR CONSUMPTIVES

FIRST FLOOR PLAN

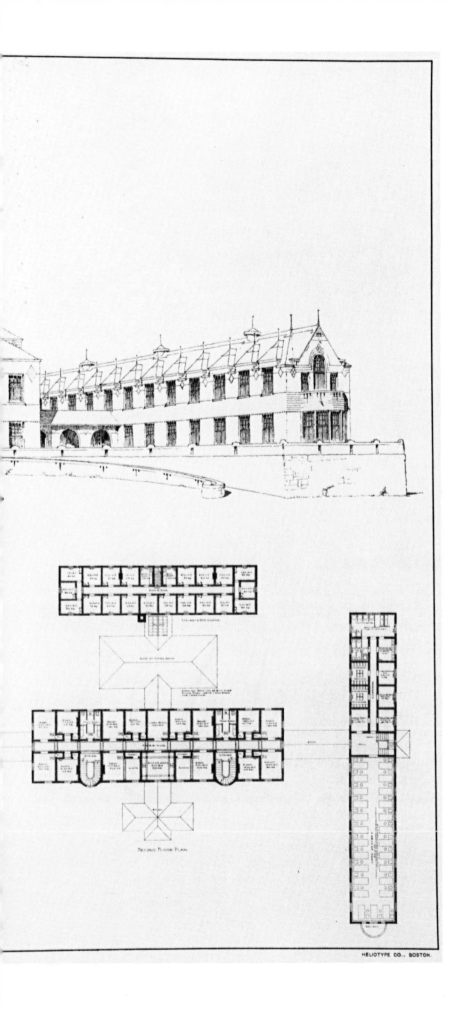

PLATE 209
"A Competitive Design for Rhode Island State Hospital for Consumptives," Smith and Walker, *American Architect and Building News*, Vol. 82, No. 1460, Dec. 19, 1903. (AIA Archives)

PLATE 210
"Red Swan Inn [Warwick,
NY]," E.G.W. Dietrich,
*Architect's and Builder's
Magazine*, Vol. 6 (37), No.
3, Dec. 1904. (AIC)

PLATE 211
"Stable of Honorable J.M.
Grosvenor Jr. [Swampscott,
MA]," Edwin J. Lewis,
*American Architect and
Building News* (Interna-
tional Edition), Vol. 89,
No. 1583, April 28, 1906.
(AIA Archives)

PLATE 212
"Residence of Samuel B.
Hubbard, Jr. [Jacksonville,
FL]," McClure and
Holmes, *Architect's and
Builder's Magazine*, Vol. 8
(29), No. 2, Nov. 1906.
(AIC)

PLATE 213
"Residence of George T.
Cochran [Los Angeles,
CA]," Train and Williams,
Western Architect, Vol. 10,
No. 1, Jan. 1907. (AIC)

PLATE 214
"Residence of Mr. H.C.
French [Pasadena, CA],"
Hudson and Munsel,
Western Architect, Vol. 20,
No. 4, April 6, 1907.
(AIC)

PLATE 215
"House of Reverand
Howard T. Mosher, Alex-
ander Street [Rochester,
NY]," Claude F. Bragdon,
*American Architect and
Building News* (Interna-
tional Edition), Vol. 91,
No. 1632, April 6, 1907.
(AIA Archives)

185

PLATE 218
"Bungalow of Mr. N.H.
Grady [Lookout Mountain,
TN]," D.V. Stroop, *Western Architect*, Vol. 20, No.
10, Oct. 1907. (AIC)

PLATE 219
"Residence for Mrs.
E. Moore [Los Angeles,
CA]," Hunt and Eager,
Western Architect, Vol. 20,
No. 12, Dec. 1907. (AIC)

PLATE 220
"Mae Cottage [Oakland,
CA]," Julia Morgan,
Inland Architect, Vol. 51,
No. 1, Jan. 1908. (AIC)

PLATE 221
"Gardener's Cottage [Dedham, MA]," Mr. A.W. Longfellow, *American Architect and Building News* (International Edition), Vol. 93, No. 1688, April 29, 1908. (AIA Archives)

PLATE 222
"Residence of Fred Weed [Winnipeg, Mantoba]," V.W. Harwood, *Western Architect*, Vol. 11, No. 5, May 1908. (AIC)

PLATE 223
"Residence at Pasadena,
CA," Greene and Greene,
Western Architect, Vol. 13,
No. 6, June 1909. (AIC)

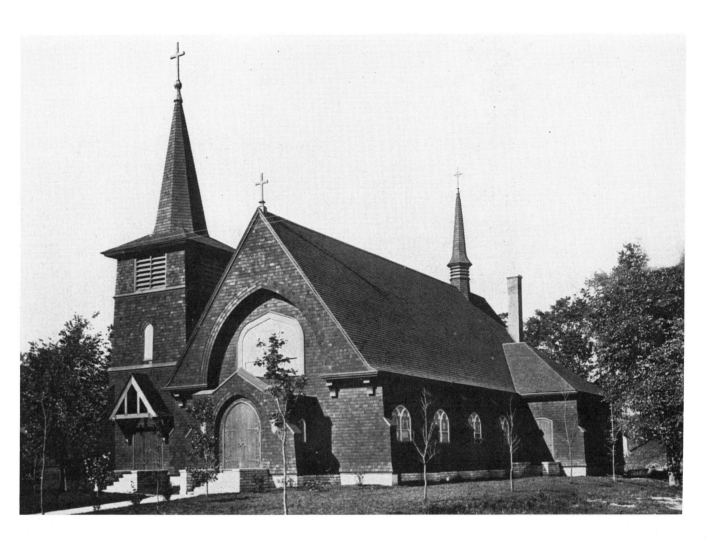

PLATE 224
"Roman Catholic Chapel
[Lenoxdale, MA]," John W.
Donahue, *Western Archi-
tect*, Vol. 14, No. 3, Sept.
1909. (AIC)

PLATE 225
"Bungalow of L. Jerome Aimar, Architect [Navesink Highlands, NJ]," *Architect's and Builder's Magazine*, Vol. 11 (42), No. 1, Nov. 1909. (AIC)

PLATE 226
"Bungalow for Mr. W.S. Ellis [Navesink Highlands, NJ]," Walter Hankin, *Architect's and Builder's Magazine*, Vol. 11 (42), No. 1, Nov. 1909. (AIC)

PLATE 227
"House of Joseph P.
Knapp, Esq. [South-
ampton, LI, NY]," John
Russell Pope, *American Ar-
chitect—The Architectural
Review*, Vol. 122, No.
2402, Sept. 13, 1922. (AIA
Archives)

Index